Astral Travel

How to Experience Astral Projection and Unlock Higher Dimensions

© Copyright 2025 - All rights reserved.

The content contained within this book may not be reproduced, duplicated, or transmitted without direct written permission from the author or the publisher.

Under no circumstances will any blame or legal responsibility be held against the publisher or author for any damages, reparation, or monetary loss due to the information contained within this book, either directly or indirectly.

Legal Notice:

This book is copyright-protected. It is only for personal use. You cannot amend, distribute, sell, use, quote, or paraphrase any part of the content within this book without the consent of the author or publisher.

Disclaimer Notice:

Please note the information contained within this document is for educational and entertainment purposes only. All effort has been executed to present accurate, up-to-date, reliable, and complete information. No warranties of any kind are declared or implied. Readers acknowledge that the author is not engaging in the rendering of legal, financial, medical, or professional advice. The content within this book has been derived from various sources. Please consult a licensed professional before attempting any techniques outlined in this book.

By reading this document, the reader agrees that under no circumstances is the author responsible for any losses, direct or indirect, that are incurred as a result of the use of the information contained within this document, including, but not limited to, errors, omissions, or inaccuracies.

Your Free Gift
(only available for a limited time)

Thanks for getting this book! If you want to learn more about various spirituality topics, then join Mari Silva's community and get a free guided meditation MP3 for awakening your third eye. This guided meditation mp3 is designed to open and strengthen ones third eye so you can experience a higher state of consciousness. Simply visit the link below the image to get started.

https://spiritualityspot.com/meditation

Or, Scan the QR code!

Table of Contents

INTRODUCTION 1
CHAPTER 1: FUNDAMENTAL CONCEPTS OF ASTRAL PROJECTION 3
CHAPTER 2: PREPARING FOR THE ASTRAL REALM I 13
CHAPTER 3: PREPARING FOR THE ASTRAL REALM II 24
CHAPTER 4: INDUCTION METHODS FOR SUCCESSFUL TRAVELS 36
CHAPTER 5: NAVIGATING THE ASTRAL PLANE 48
CHAPTER 6: HEALING THROUGH THE ASTRAL 60
CHAPTER 7: CONNECTING WITH SPIRIT GUIDES AND HIGHER BEINGS 72
CHAPTER 8: COMING HOME FROM ASTRAL TRAVEL 84
CHAPTER 9: CULTIVATING A LIFELONG JOURNEY OF EXPLORATION 95
CONCLUSION 104
HERE'S ANOTHER BOOK BY MARI SILVA THAT YOU MIGHT LIKE 107
YOUR FREE GIFT (ONLY AVAILABLE FOR A LIMITED TIME) ... 108
REFERENCES 109
IMAGE SOURCES 115

Introduction

Between 8 and 10 percent of individuals claim to have experienced an out-of-body experience at least once in their lives. An out-of-body experience occurs when your spirit, consciousness, or astral body steps outside your physical body. These experiences often take place during sleep or under sleep hypnosis. However, avid practitioners of astral projection master the ability to swing among the states of consciousness while simply relaxing and meditating.

The idea that people can exit their bodies when they are in a dream-like state dates back to ancient times. Ancient Egyptian hieroglyphs, Hindu scripture, and records of ancient Chinese practices reference concepts like the exiting or travel of the soul and silver cord, which are the essence of the modern-day understanding of astral travel. Numerous shamans and those with New Age beliefs think that vivid dreams and visions they get during their out-of-body experiences allow them to communicate with cosmic intelligence.

You can learn a lot about the universe and yourself through astral projection. Unsurprisingly, as spiritual topics for self-improvement, like manifestation, gained more popularity over the past few years, astral projection has also recently begun to attract much interest and attention. When used correctly, this tool can help you transform your life and work toward becoming the best version of yourself.

This book will serve as your go-to guide for exploring the world of astral travel. It features in-depth yet easy-to-follow knowledge and a wide array of practical exercises, making it suitable for beginners and advanced practitioners. This book is written by an astral travel and projection expert who will explain how to use the knowledge and techniques to achieve personal growth and healing, practice spiritual communication, and work on self-discovery.

Here, you will learn, in-depth, what astral projection is, what happens to your astral and physical bodies in the process and gain some historical background into this practice. You will learn how to develop the skills needed to master this practice and dive into induction methods to successfully achieve an out-of-body experience. You will learn how to explore the astral realm, manage the aftermath of astral travel, and integrate the practice into your life safely and effectively. Each chapter includes practical exercises that will help you put the information it offers into practice. Move on to the first chapter to start your journey of transforming your life through astral projection!

Chapter 1: Fundamental Concepts of Astral Projection

This chapter explores the concept of astral projection, its history, benefits, spiritual implications, and much more. Reading it, you will learn about consciousness, energy layers, and everything you need to know to prepare for the practical application of astral travel you will read about in further chapters.

What Is Astral Projection?

Astral projection has been defined in several ways by diverse cultures. Most agree, however, that it involves the spiritual body (the astral body) separating itself from the physical body, traveling near and far, and providing an out-of-body experience. While this experience can look different for practitioners, it comes with a raised awareness – which is why it differs from dreams and similar spiritual practices involving an altered state of consciousness.

Astral projections are like having an out-of-body experience.[1]

People can astral travel as far as they want. For example, you may not even leave the room where your physical body is located or feel like you have traveled much further. In the first case, you are likely to have a stronger awareness of your physical body and everything happening around it. By traveling further, you will be more focused on exploring the setting you have found yourself in. This can be another part of the physical world or another world altogether.

During astral travel, you will remain fully conscious of your physical body and feel like you are floating. You feel relaxed while your spirit wanders, exploring whatever place it is channeled toward.

At other times, practitioners describe astral travel as visits to another realm, which may look very similar to the physical realm. Still, in most cases, this is a spiritual realm with a different energy signature, presenting plenty of wisdom to be gathered for those who seek it. Voluntarily traveling often involves purposely choosing the spiritual realm as a destination for astral projection.

Why does astral travel take people to the spiritual realm? The astral body consists of energy or, more precisely, it represents spiritual energy. It can forge a connection to the spiritual world even involuntarily and take you there, floating through space and time.

According to many experienced practitioners, the spiritual realm has several layers or dimensions, each representing a location and a collection of astral matters (energy, wisdom, beings, etc.). When exploring the layers of the astral realm, you may experience changes every time you visit them. Besides actual changes in the energy, this may happen because your perception of them changes; thus, what you see is different.

When Does Astral Projection Occur?

Astral travel can happen voluntarily and involuntarily. For example, many people experience a short out-of-body experience before falling asleep, not realizing they are astral projecting. You may be aware that you're lying on your bed and everything you did before lying down, but now you feel separated from your body. You may even be able to look down on yourself while you're falling asleep. With practice, you can take this to the level of observing yourself from above your physical body.

People who experience near-death or otherwise frightening experiences or who have felt a connection to deceased loved ones have also described short bursts of astral travel. It may feel like a loss of control over the body, with an enhanced focus on what's happening with the spirit.

Spiritual healers, shamans, and other practitioners can voluntarily use astral projection – after lots of practice to avoid losing control and having uncontrolled out-of-body experiences.

Lucid dreaming is another example of astral projection that can happen voluntarily or involuntarily. During this experience, a person is aware of their conscious memories while indulging in an experience that opens a new world to them. Unlike regular dreams, the world of lucid dreaming feels different because you have more control over the entire experience. In the voluntary version, you can focus on specific aspects of your surroundings and the experience is not limited to what your dreams are trying to show you.

How Does Consciousness Work?

You may be wondering how consciousness can be manipulated in a way that it separates itself from the physical body. Human beings have physical and non-physical components. As its name implies, the physical body represents the physical component, and so does the brain itself.

While governed by the brain, the mind bridges physical and non-physical components, including the spirit. The spirit is often described as a set of values, choices, and information a person gathers throughout their life (or lives, depending on which belief system they go by).

In many cultures and belief systems, the spirit lives separately from the physical components, allowing it to leave it and cross time and space during and after the physical body's life.

From a psychological standpoint, consciousness is the awareness of a person's experiences, including past and current emotions, thoughts, and their relationship to situations. In other words, your consciousness makes you aware of your environment in a unique way. How you describe something in your consciousness will always differ from how another person may define the same thing. Your perspective is different, so what you see is individual to you.

Psychologists and spiritual practitioners identify various states of consciousness, from dreams to meditative states to the states that are altered by mental health conditions or psychoactive substances. These states have functions ranging from allowing you to control your thoughts, feelings, and actions to decision-making, priority setting, and information processing to learning and adapting to new circumstances.

Before becoming a heavily researched state in psychology, philosophers had already examined consciousness deeply. For example, Rene Descartes developed the concept of the body being separate from the mind while simultaneously interacting.

Rene Descartes.[1]

Neuroscientists and psychologists have developed several theories about consciousness, including the global workspace theory, integrated information theory, predictive processing theories, and higher-order theories.

The global workspace theory is based on the existence of an information database within the brain. A person uses information from this database to build their awareness of themselves and the world around them. This theory offers a broader understanding of consciousness and its importance in spiritual practices. To simplify how the global workspace works, you can imagine it as a large theater. You choose what you bring to the stage, which is your consciousness. To fill the stage with actors, set pieces, lights, etc., you keep reaching into this database of information until you have created the scene that fits your purpose.

The integration information theory focuses more on the neurobiological function of consciousness, providing a peek into the physical process that helps form your conscious experiences. How successful you will be at expanding your consciousness and using it in spiritual practices (including astral travel) depends on how the physical parts work together. Each helps harness and create bits of information that become integrated into a joint experience. According to this theory, experiences can be conscious to different degrees, with some experiences closer to conscious awareness than others. When more parts work together to integrate information, the experience will be closer to conscious awareness. This theory explains the unique nuances between the quality of human experiences.

The highly developed brain regions are at the core of predictive processing theories. These regions allocate information and context to other regions and help to interpret the information the brain receives from the senses. The senses provide information about the environment, which the brain uses to predict and process the experience, forming conscious awareness of it.

Higher-order theories claim that consciousness is formed from information gathered from the low-order perceptions (senses) and then processed by the high-order centers of the brain. Similar to previous theories, these connect the neurobiological components of the brain with experiences representing the foundation of conscious awareness.

The Seven Energy Layers

The energy body (the subtle or astral body) is a crucial aspect of astral travel. Its physical representation is the aura, a sometimes visible and colorful layer of energy around the human body.

The aura is a collection of a person's entire energy. That person's energetic health determines its color, shape, and dimensions. The aura is a good indicator of health and a great way to gauge someone's ability to perform spiritual practices.

The aura is a collection of a person's energy.[a]

The aura and the energy body have seven layers, each of which plays a role in spiritual work, including astral travel. These seven layers allow you to separate your consciousness from your physical body and journey across space and time.

The seven energy layers are as follows:
1. **Etheric:** The layer with the most concentrated energy, storing most of the person's vital essence. It is linked to the sacral chakra and the physical body itself. Being closest to the physical body, it draws energy and information from every cell, tissue, and organ.
2. **Emotional:** The emotional layer is connected to desires, the sense of self, and feelings. You either control it or let it take control over

you. This layer is also associated with memories and information your spirit carries from other lives.

3. **Mental:** Above the emotional layer lies the ever-changing mental layer. Associated with the throat and solar plexus chakra, it is a bridge between thoughts and feelings. It contains every piece of information you learn and every thought process you develop.

4. **Astral:** Connected to the heart chakra, the astral layer is associated with love. It also connects to the chakras closest to the physical body and the ones tied to the spiritual being. Hence, it is one of the most important layers for expanding your consciousness in the realm of astral projection.

5. **Spiritual:** When you sense something from your environment, the spiritual layer is the first one you reach into to determine how you perceive what you are sensing. It contains information about what you have previously learned as well as elements of your personality and spirit. All this data will determine your perception and whether you trust it.

6. **Celestial:** This layer of inner feelings is also linked to a higher purpose, goals, and inspiration. It can also connect to other spiritual entities and draw energy from the environment. Noble feelings like gratitude, honor, and respect emerge from this layer before reaching full consciousness.

7. **Ketheric:** Associated with the crown chakra, this is the ultimate layer of consciousness. Here, your universal energy gathers, allowing your awareness to rise to its highest level – and even expand with practice. This layer also stores the information you harness during your astral journeys.

What Are the Benefits of Astral Travel?

Your astral journey can take you wherever you want to go without having to physically move, which is one of the major benefits of astral travel. Unlike other spiritual practices, you will not be limited in your exploration. You can revisit past events or explore places you always wanted to explore. Whether you have visited them or not, or whether you have been present in the past event or not, it does not matter. With astral travel, you can go there and explore to your heart's content.

It takes a little practice, but once you get the hang of it, you will be able to direct your travel consciously, do what you want, and see, hear, or sense whatever you want to explore. You can traverse space and time if you adequately prepare for your journey.

You remain connected to your physical body despite traveling as far as to other realms. More importantly, your energy remains attached to your body, allowing you to control everything together. It can also help you to learn more about yourself. As you expand the boundaries of your astral projection abilities, you will discover more and more about the connection between the physical and non-physical components of your being.

If you want to learn more about all other dimensions out there, astral travel will allow you to do this. You will no longer be confined to the physical dimension (the one surrounding your physical body) but can immerse yourself in spiritual and emotional dimensions.

Astral travel also allows you to meet the inhabitants of other realms, connect spiritually, and learn from them. Those who want to remain connected to their ancestors or deceased loved ones sometimes use astral travel to communicate with spirits that have passed on after the passing of their physical bodies.

Astral projection can be a wonderful tool for personal growth. It allows you to explore, learn, expand, evolve, and become the person you wish to be. How? While traveling, you will have to control your thoughts, allowing you to train them to channel your emotions and intentions.

By learning to control your thoughts during astral travel, you can manifest your intentions during spiritual practice and day-to-day life. Energy moves more freely through the astral planes (as opposed to the physical plane, where it runs into obstacles all the time), which also helps manifest your intentions more easily.

Lastly, another massive benefit you gain from astral travel is that when you are finally reunited with your physical body, you can recall everything you saw, sensed, and learned during your journey. You can explore the entire universe with your imagination and energy and create memories that will serve you for a lifetime and may serve your spirit in other lives.

Examples from History

There have been countless examples of people experiencing astral travel throughout history. People have been practicing it since the beginning of time, with some of the most notable mentions coming from religious texts like the Quran. The Quran describes the Prophet Muhammad using astral travel as part of his voyage from Mecca to Jerusalem and later to the heavens.

Prophets of Native American tribes were also believed to be able to traverse back and forth between the spiritual world and the mortal world via astral projection. Likewise, the shamans of some Indigenous communities of the Amazon region were known to have used astral travel to join themselves with their deities and absorb their power. They called these "soul flights," which is a great way to describe astral travel.

According to Japanese legends, when a person holds a grudge against another, they can experience Ikiryō, a burst of astral projection to the other person's location. The spontaneous appearance lasts for a very short time but can be repeated depending on whether the conflict between the two people is resolved or not.

Ancient Egyptians were equally fascinated by the concept of astral travel. They defined the astral body as "Ka" and claimed that the person's energy (and spirit) can separate from their physical body and explore the spiritual plane by hovering from place to place.

Hindu texts similarly describe the astral body – the part of the human being that can travel to and engage with higher planes of existence. In Buddhism, monks are also believed to achieve the spiritual fulfillment called nirvana through astral travel.

Interest in astral travel surged during the Victorian era when people sought various methods to reach a higher level of consciousness and have out-of-body experiences. In the 19th century, mystics recognized the benefits of astral projection and integrated it into their spiritual practices.

One of the pioneers who popularized astral projection was Helena Blavatsky, the founder of the Theosophical Society, built on the mystical system of Theosophy. Her teachings included introducing energy layers, the astral body, and exploring the astral planes.

Astral Projection Checklist

Wondering if learning how to astral travel is right for you? Here is a quick checklist to find out:

- You want to remove fear and resistance from opening your mind to spiritual practices.
- You want to train your awareness and bring it to a higher level.
- You want to learn an efficient mind-clearing practice.
- You want to widen your perspectives.
- You want to practice visualization.
- You want to exercise patience in spiritual practices.
- You want to reach an emotional, spiritual, or psychological breakthrough.
- You want to strengthen and combine various psychic abilities.

If you check over half of the items on the list, you will benefit massively from practicing astral projection.

Chapter 2: Preparing for the Astral Realm I

This chapter serves as your go-to guide for preparing for the astral realm. Here, you will learn how to set up and clear your space, get into the right mental headspace, and set and focus on your intentions for out-of-body experiences. You will also learn to practice meditation and visualization and keep a dream journal to aid your astral projection efforts.

You will learn tips on using the REM sleep cycle to induce the mental state needed for this spiritual endeavor, what to do if you do not get it right first, and how to return to your body afterward. Finally, you will find a list of daily affirmations to repeat and tips on eating and fueling your body.

Set up Your Space

Find a relaxing space where you can rest comfortably without interruption for at least an hour. This area should be calming and free of distractions or stimulants. Dim the lights, use soft cushions, play white noise or calming music, burn incense, and ensure the temperature is neither too hot nor too cold. Creating the ideal atmosphere will make it easier to relax and focus on drifting into the state needed for astral projection rather than becoming distracted by physical sensations and discomfort.

Try Aromatherapy

Try aromatherapy to transcend.'

- **Frankincense:** This is among the most popular essential oils in spiritual practices due to its ability to induce relaxation and meditative states. It can bring balance, clarity, and peace to the mind, allowing you to achieve deeper spiritual understanding.
- **Lavender:** This essential oil is renowned for its calming and relaxing properties. Incorporating it into your life can make you more gentle, tender, and compassionate, as it can help release heavy, unwanted emotions.
- **Clary Sage:** This essential oil can help you navigate and overcome extreme life transitions, become more centered and balanced, and manage symptoms like lethargy and mood swings.
- **Sandalwood:** This essential oil can help clear emotions that prevent you from achieving a relaxed and meditative state. It can also calm your nerves and stabilize your emotions. It is a popular tool used to heal the heart chakra and stabilize emotions.

Space Clearing Tips

- **Smudging**: This widely used space-clearing method involves burning herbs like cedar, palo santo, and sage. Burning these herbs can purify the surrounding energy and clear the space of negative influences. You can either light up loose herbs or a herb bundle, allowing the smoke to spread into the room. Make sure you focus on windows, corners, and doorways, as these are often the harbors and entryways of negative energy. Set the intention to clear the space beforehand, do not leave the burning herbs unattended, and keep them away from flammable materials.

Smudging purifies your surroundings.[5]

- **Sound Cleansing**: Use bells, singing bowls, or chimes to generate vibrations that will clear the negative energy in your space. Move around as you create these sounds, allowing the sound to resonate and fill each room.
- **Clear With Nature**: To clear the space's energy, allow sunlight and fresh air to flow in. Plants can also have a cleansing and energizing effect.

Get into the Right Mental Headspace

Spiritual endeavors, just like any other undertakings in life, require a level of faith and self-assurance. Doubting yourself and questioning your ability to unlock higher states of consciousness can block you from succeeding. To get into the right mental headspace, consider saying positive affirmations and truly believing that you are capable of astral projection even if you have no prior experience or have failed in the past. Keep in mind that you may not successfully achieve an out-of-body experience the first time around. Even if you do everything by the book and follow all the steps to a T, you may struggle during your first few attempts. Most importantly, keep trying, stay patient, positive, and faithful.

Set and Focus on Your Intention

You must set your intention and focus on it before trying astral projection. Intention offers a sense of clarity and direction and is crucial to staying safe throughout the practice. The astral plane is an unknown territory, which can feel unsettling the first few times around. Navigating it without intent and purpose can make you feel lost and cause you to wander aimlessly in a realm that you are unfamiliar with.

Once you drift off into that state of consciousness without purpose, you will not know what you are doing there or what you want to achieve from that experience, which can trigger fear and anxiety. Fear, feeling overwhelmed, and disorientation can create a negative experience, making it difficult to get into the right mindset needed for astral projection. They can also abruptly bring you out of projection, which can feel unsettling. Panic and anxiety can hinder your ability to smoothly return to your body as well. However, remember that feeling stuck in the astral realm is not dangerous and is only temporary.

Setting your intention and focusing on it is essential to having a positive astral projection experience. It also serves as an anchor for your thoughts and practice, allowing you to stay concentrated throughout the experience. Knowing what you want to achieve by astral projection aligns your mental, emotional, and spiritual energy with that goal, which helps dissipate feelings of doubt, fear, and subconscious resistance.

Whether you want to communicate with spirits, find answers, or simply explore other realms, keep your purpose in mind as you prepare for and navigate the astral world. Call upon your guardian angels, spirit guides, or the higher power you are working with, and ask them to protect you and your energy as you embark on this journey. You can also visualize a white, protective circle of light as you prepare for this practice.

Practice Meditation

Meditative practices allow you to relax mentally and physically. Meditation helps you to stay focused on the present instead of ruminating on the past or worrying about the future. This allows you to direct your energy, focus, and intention toward preparing for astral projection. Meditation sounds easier said than done, especially if you have not practiced it before. Many people struggle to stay still for prolonged periods. Others struggle with the inability to keep their thoughts at bay, and some struggle with both.

Meditation allows you to relax your body and your mind.'

Start by meditating for a few minutes daily, focusing on doing it right. Get into a comfortable position and concentrate on the present moment. Purposefully become aware of your body's different sensations at that moment. If intrusive thoughts arise, acknowledge their presence and visualize them floating away and out of your brain. Avoid interacting with or judging these thoughts. Gradually increase your practice time as you grow more comfortable with it. You can also look up guided meditation videos or audio to help ease you into it.

When meditating, it is always good to set your intention beforehand. In this way, you have an anchor to keep you grounded throughout. If you feel bored, feel compelled to move, or experience intrusive thoughts, redirecting your thoughts toward your intention will allow you to remember the purpose of your practice and encourage you to return to it with better focus, drive, and clarity.

Not all your meditation sessions will be equally as fruitful. There will be days when you will feel like you are making great progress and others when you will struggle to set a single thought aside. Always remember that progress is not linear and consider experimenting with different methods that can help enhance your experience. For instance, some people find it easier to meditate when they have binaural beats or white noise playing in the background. Test different sounds at different volumes, the effects of burning various incense and essential oils, and dimming the lights or using candles until you determine the environment that you find most conducive to meditation.

Once you dive into a meditative state, bring your attention to each part of your body separately. First, notice how your feet feel. Then, bring your attention to your calves, working your way up to your head. Not only does this help to train your thoughts, but it also helps you relax and channel your body's positive energy. Each body part is associated with a different chakra or energy point. As you bring your attention to your head, feel the air rejuvenating your body every time you inhale, and tell yourself that your body is relaxing as you exhale. Feel the vibration covering and rippling through your body with every breath.

Keep a Dream Journal

Keeping a dream journal can help you boost your awareness and develop the skills needed to effectively practice astral projection. Every morning, dedicate a few minutes to recalling and reflecting on your dreams as soon as you wake up. It may be very challenging at first, especially when you wake up and feel like you have not even dreamt at all. There will come moments when you give up without making any progress. Dream recall can take months of practice and dedication. The longer you preserve, the better you will train your mind to remember your dreams and other nocturnal experiences more vividly.

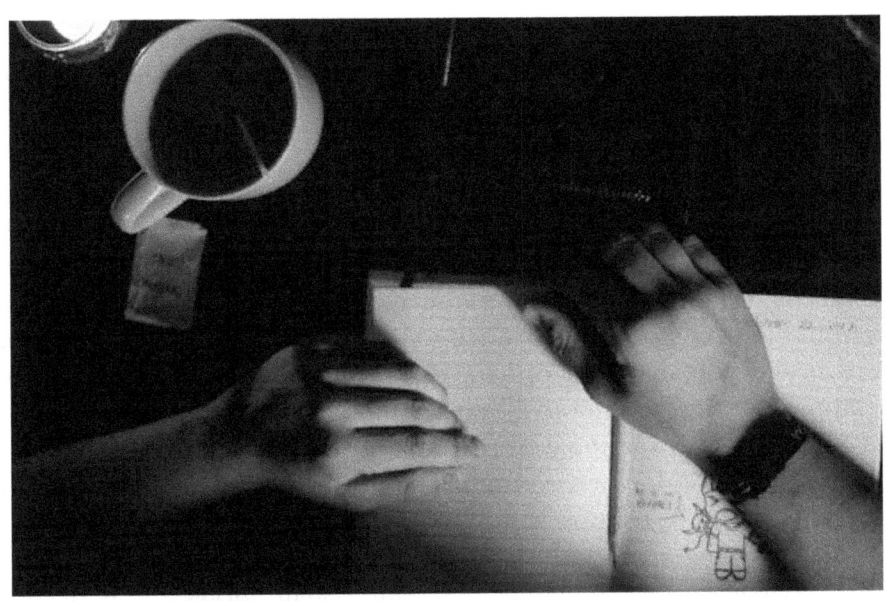

Keeping a dream journal will allow you to tap into altered states of consciousness in more detail.[7]

Like sleep, astral projection is an altered state of consciousness. Learning to recall your dreams will prepare you to remember your astral experiences. If you cannot recall them, you will not benefit from them, which puts all your other efforts to waste. Over time, keeping a dream journal will bring your attention to the smallest subtleties of your altered states of consciousness. Keeping track of these nuances, whether you experience them in your dreams or during your astral projections, will make you aware of any recurrent symbols, patterns, and themes about your life, thoughts, feelings, and subconscious. The subtleties can also help you differentiate between your dreams, lucid dreams, and astral projections.

Incorporating dream journaling into your routine emphasizes the importance of experiencing and recalling altered states of consciousness in your brain. When your intent to interact with these realities is reinforced, it becomes a lot easier to drift into these states. Keeping track of your progress can also boost your confidence in your own ability to practice. Being more confident makes you more relaxed yet focused, which is the ideal mental state needed for astral projection.

Practice Visualization

Visualization is another invaluable tool that can help you prepare for astral projection. It can give you insight into what you are going to see and experience on your journey, relieving some of your worries and anxieties. When practicing visualization, try to imagine that all your awareness comes from your third-eye chakra, which is located in the center of your forehead.

Close your eyes and imagine yourself floating outside of your body and traveling into the astral realm. Picture your room, yourself, and your surroundings with as much detail as possible. Direct your focus toward one specific point and fixate on the image of yourself. See yourself how you would look right now. Consider your position, what you are wearing, where exactly you are sitting or lying down, and how the chair, pillows, or bed appear under your body. You should feel as if your soul has left your body and is observing it from above. If you cannot do that, you can try the rope method, where you imagine that a rope is hanging from the ceiling, and you are using it to pull yourself out of your body. Visualize yourself exploring an unknown world and meeting new beings. Get as creative as you wish, and make sure your visualizations are as detailed and vivid as possible. Try to capture the thoughts and feelings you would have if your visualizations were true. This can set you up for a successful out-of-body experience.

Visualizing the experience can condition your mind and body for the real thing. It is a chance to rehearse the feeling of being in the astral realm, which can make you feel more at ease. It is also an opportunity to align more with your intention and better understand why you want to embark on this journey. Visualization also signals to your subconscious mind that you are prepared and ready for astral projection, making your attempts more effective.

Return to Your Body

When you are ready to return, gently redirect your focus to your body. Notice how your limbs feel on the surface beneath you, or try to wiggle your toes or fingers. Bring your attention to anything in your body that can help you return to the present moment. Some people find it helpful to think or say, "I call my energy back."

Regain Your Consciousness and Reflect

Once you fully regain your consciousness, relax and reflect on what happened. After processing your trip to the astral realm, write about it in your dream journal. Take notes on remarkable occurrences or themes that came up, and any lessons you have learned. Familiarizing yourself with the process makes it a lot easier to drift into and out of your astral projections over time.

What if You Can't Do It?

Most people cannot successfully astral project on their first few attempts, so do not worry if you fail. Do not give up if you fall asleep in the process, cannot get yourself into the right mental state, or struggle with clear visualization.

If it gets too frustrating, you may convince yourself that astral projection is not for you. However, remember that this thought can block you from achieving the mental state needed for astral projection. Everyone is capable of astral projection if they put their heart and mind into it. While it comes more naturally to some people than others, you will eventually get there if you keep practicing.

There is no need to rush the process. You do not have a timeline and are not competing with yourself or others. If you feel discouraged, take a step back and relax. Connect with yourself and become attuned to your surroundings. Remember that you can achieve remarkable things. Reflect on all the things you have achieved and that you are proud of. Your ability to astral project is not a reflection of your ability.

Trust that your astral projections will become more vivid with practice and teach you deeper, more meaningful lessons that change your perspective on life. Astral projections can alter your subconscious, changing the way you think and approach different situations. It also boosts your consciousness and makes you feel more at peace in your daily interactions. While you may be keen on experiencing the benefits of astral projection, do not treat it like a chore. Do not forget to have fun and lean into your curiosity during your trips to the astral realm.

Using the REM Sleep Cycle for Astral Projection

Astral projection relies highly on your REM, or Rapid-Eye Movement, sleep cycles. These are the same sleep cycles that trigger dreams. Your brain is active during REM sleep, showcasing similar activity to when awake. You are not deeply asleep during the REM phase of the sleep cycle, making it conducive for out-of-body experiences. Astral projection and similar experiences are most likely to occur when you are in the mental state of being between asleep and awake.

To induce this state, you need to relax your mind and body as much as you can, allowing yourself to fall half-asleep. When you notice that you are drifting off, focus on how you feel mentally instead of your physical sensations. The trick is to fight the urge to fall deeply asleep and stay hyper-aware of the vibrations surrounding you. Align your body with these vibrations, allowing them to overtake your subtle body, causing it to float off the physical. Picture each limb as it leaves your body, one at a time. All your focus at this moment should be directed toward floating your astral body out of your physical body.

Daily Affirmations for Astral Projection

- My mind and body are ready for astral projection.
- I am at peace and fully relaxed.
- I am naturally at peace and relaxed.
- I am capable of achieving astral projection.
- I enjoy having out-of-body experiences.
- It's easy for me to leave my physical body.
- My mind is aware yet calm.
- I am attuned to my astral body.
- My astral body is leaving my physical body.
- The ability to astral project comes naturally to me.
- Astral projection is a natural aspect of my life.
- I am mentally, emotionally, and spiritually prepared for astral projection.
- I am capable of inducing out-of-body experiences.
- I am safe and protected.
- My consciousness is safely open to the astral plane.
- I am in a state of utter relaxation and peace.
- I am always opening and expanding my awareness.

Alkaline Nutrition and Astral Projection

Keeping an alkaline body can promote relaxation by reducing stress, acidity, and anxiety. This can help you with your meditation efforts and help you ease into the mindset required for astral projection. It can also increase the energy flow in your body, improve your mental clarity, and reduce emotions that block you from embarking on out-of-body experiences.

Tips for Increasing Alkalinity in the Body:

- Use alkaline drinks, such as water infused with honey, turmeric, cinnamon, and lemon juice.
- Eat a plant-based diet, and avoid acidic, processed, and spicy foods.
- Limit non-vegetarian foods, as these are harder to digest and can lower your vibrational energy.
- Focus on healing your gut and ensure that you digest your food properly and that you regularly eliminate toxins from your body.
- Eat in moderation. Smaller balanced meals throughout the day can boost your energy and avoid feelings of sluggishness following heavy meals.

Now that you have read this chapter, you have learned almost everything you need to know about preparing for the astral realm. The next chapter will delve deeper into the physical, mental, and emotional groundwork necessary for a successful astral projection practice.

Chapter 3: Preparing for the Astral Realm II

This chapter lays the groundwork for successfully executing astral projection. It tackles physical, mental, and emotional preparation as the training steps to make astral travel easier for beginners. These steps include energy channeling, relaxation, mind-clearing, and much more.

Basic Meditative Practices

Basic meditative exercises will help you to calm your body and mind, centering the latter to become more aware of your surroundings.

Meditation to Reach a Hypnagogic State

When you reach a hypnagogic state, you become fully relaxed while remaining consciously aware of everything happening in and around you.

You can practice meditation on a chair if needed.'

Instructions:
1. Sit with your back straight on a chair or cross-legged against the wall. Keep your head straight with your gaze focused on a point straight ahead.
2. Look at your surroundings.
3. Bring your awareness to your neck muscles, tense them, and let them relax. Repeat this pattern with all the major muscle groups in your body.
4. Breathe normally and notice how your belly expands. If it only inflates slightly, try deepening your breaths to breathe more deeply through your belly. Take long breaths and allow your stomach to expand fully.
5. When you reach a natural, deep breathing rhythm, close your eyes.
6. Breathing deeply, visualize the point you were staring at before you closed your eyes. At this point, you may become distracted with thoughts like "What am I doing?" or "I forgot ...." Let these go and bring your awareness back to the image you have created in your mind.
7. Slowly, your mind will clear of unhelpful thoughts, and you will go deeper and deeper into the space where it can focus on the present and whatever image you want it to conjure during projection.

Additional Techniques to Induce the Hypnagogic State

The beauty of hypnagogic meditation is that it does not have to be one standalone exercise. It can be a continuous stream of actions performed throughout the day, preparing you to immerse into a deeply relaxed yet hyperaware state.

Instructions:
1. When you have a few minutes to rest (whether it is to take a nap or simply when you do not have anything else to do) throughout the day, create the intention to induce a hypnagogic state. How? Think about a position that helps you relax (for example, one you assume just before falling asleep). The goal is to trick your mind into thinking that it can fully relax but remain aware of any image it may create.
2.

3. Take a few minutes to relax, breathing deeply through your nostrils and exhaling through your mouth. Continue breathing until you feel tension leaving your body.
4. Want to test if you are in a hypnagogic state? Try creating some random images in your mind. If you are successful and the images that pop up are random, your mind is clear and relaxed. The images should not be forced or directed by any thoughts. If they are, you will need to continue relaxing.
5. As you do these short meditations throughout the day, continue focusing on generating random images. Sometimes, they will be accompanied by thoughts and emotions, and that is okay. Simply observe them with curiosity and let them go without judgment.

Deep Breathing Exercises

Deep breathing exercises work wonders for calming your mind and body. They also open up your consciousness, making you more receptive to any information you will gather during projection.

Simple Breathing

Instructions:

1. Get comfortable, close your eyes, and start deepening your breathing.
2. As you do, notice how taking deeper breaths makes you feel. Notice becoming relaxed until you are almost in a sleep-like state.
3. Continue breathing for 5-10 minutes or until you feel sufficiently relaxed.

Holotropic Breath

Instructions:

1. Relax and start taking deeper but quicker breaths.
2. Do not hold your breath. Simply let the big bursts of air expand your belly.
3. After a while, you will notice a change in your consciousness. You will become more aware of your body and surroundings and open to new experiences.
4. Start with a quick 5-minute session, as this breathing pattern can be exhausting. As you become more comfortable with the technique, increase the duration.

Box Breathing
Instructions:
1. Start by relaxing and imagining a box or square in front of you for a more controlled deep breathing technique.
2. As you inhale, count to four and imagine tracing the side of the square.
3. Then, as you exhale, count to four again and actually trace the bottom of the square this time.
4. Inhale again, counting to four and tracing the other side of the square.
5. Lastly, exhale again, counting to four and tracing the top of the square.
6. Repeat these steps, tracing the four lines of the square while counting to four at each inhale and exhale.
7. Continue tracing the square until your mind becomes clear and your body is relaxed enough to make separating the two easier.

Visualization Exercises

Visualization is a helpful first step when preparing for the separation during projection attempts. It helps you train your focus and channel your intention. You can start with a simple exercise, like visualizing an empty glass.

Simple Visualization
Instructions:
1. Sit down and place the object (for example, the empty glass) on the table in front of you. Then, take a good look at it.
2. Then, close your eyes and try to see the glass in your mind, just like you did with your eyes open. Try to create as lifelike an image as possible and hold onto it.
3. In the beginning, you may notice the image fading quickly from your mind. This is normal. When it happens, open your eyes and look at the glass again. Close your eyes and visualize the glass again.
4. If your mind starts to wander and you lose focus, channel it back to the image of the glass.

5. What if you were to rotate the glass? What would it look like? Imagine doing this in your mind. If you have trouble doing this, open your eyes, rotate the glass physically, and you'll have an image you can try to recreate.
6. When you feel confident in visualizing the object in front of you, switch to something you do not currently have in front of you but see every day. For example, you can recall the image of the candle sitting on your desk. Imagine standing right in front of it – see how big it is relative to the desk and notice its color and shape.
7. Continue this exercise to strengthen your ability to create and retain clear images in your mind.

Deeper Visualization

Once you feel confident in your ability to visualize simple objects, you can move on to larger items and even people.

Instructions:

1. Take a deep breath, relax, and imagine standing in front of your house's doorway. Focus on an object, such as a window, the color of the building, the doorknob, or the door itself. Enter the house in your mind.
2. See all the objects in the room you have entered. (Like in the previous exercise, you can start creating this image by walking through your house before you begin the visualization.) Take your time to recall your surroundings.
3. Imagine finding friends and family in the house. You can do this by starting with one person at your first attempt. Create a detailed image of their person. For example, you can do this as if describing them to someone else. How tall are they? What color is their hair? What are they wearing? Describe the shape of their face. What are they doing? Try to recall as many details as possible.

Chakra Visualization

How can visualization prepare for your astral adventures? It does that by clearing out your chakras and empowering your energy body.

Instructions:

1. Get comfortable by sitting on a chair.
2. Take a few deep breaths, close your eyes, and imagine a glowing energy ball descending onto the top of your head.

3. See this energy ball enter your crown chakra and then move down your body, passing through each energy center along the way.
4. Feel yourself relaxing under the influence of this clearing energy source.

4-7-8 Breath

This specific deep breathing exercise will calm your body and mind in a relatively short period of time.

Instructions:
1. Make yourself comfortable (you can sit or lie down) and gently close your eyes.
2. Place your tongue on the back of your top teeth.
3. Take several long, deep breaths through your nostrils.
4. Then, as you take your next breath, count to four.
5. Hold your breath until you count to seven, then release the air from your lungs while counting to eight.
6. Do not worry if you cannot do the required count in the first few tries. Practice until you can. You may feel a little lightheaded if you are not accustomed to deep breathing. This feeling will pass with practice as your body gets used to greater oxygen intake.
7. Repeat the four-seven-eight breathing pattern up to seven times. As you do, observe any thoughts that emerge in your mind. Acknowledge them and let them pass through your awareness.
8. When you feel relaxed, take a few more deep breaths without counting and allow your breathing to return to its natural rhythm.
9. Open your eyes, but continue sitting quietly for a moment.

The Body Scan

A simple body scan exercise will always feel relaxing and help you channel your focus when practicing astral projection. For the best results, do this for at least 30 minutes while preparing for astral travel.

Instructions:
1. Lie down, take a few breaths, and close your eyes (this helps you channel your mind) – or leave them open with your gaze unfocused.

2. Imagine an orb of golden light descending upon you, enveloping you with soothing energy. Feel your muscles relax under its influence.
3. As you gently breathe in and out, notice the pressure or any other sensation in your body where it touches the floor. Spend a few minutes investigating each area of contact.
4. When you feel ready, take a deep breath and focus on the part of your body you want to examine (one that does not touch the floor this time). For example, you could choose the top of your head or the upper part of your feet. Choosing a body part at one end will help you perform a systemic scan through the next steps.
5. What do you feel in this body part? Is it tingling, tightness, hot, cold, or buzzing? Is it similar to what you have felt in the contact points? You may also notice the lack of sensation. This is normal, too. Just make sure to be aware of it.
6. Whatever you notice or do not notice in the first body part, acknowledge it and let it go without judgment. Then, let the soothing energy of the golden light wash over that body part.
7. Continue exploring each body part (if you start with your head, go toward your feet, and vice versa) until the light permeates every cell, tissue, and organ in your body. As you do, remain open about what sensation you may encounter. Sometimes, they may surprise you.
8. As you explore, always release the focus of attention from one area intentionally before moving on to the next. As you practice, you may notice that your attention will wander. This is normal, too. Over time, you will learn to remain focused on where you need it for as long as needed.
9. If you notice your attention leaving you, gently channel it back (do not try to force it, as this can make you feel uneasy, and it will not help your preparation). By redirecting it repeatedly, you are training it to work for you.
10. After scanning and relaxing your entire body, spend a few moments focusing on how it feels. Do you feel like a weight has been lifted? Do you feel like you can breathe more freely? Perhaps you do not feel limited or distracted by tension anymore.

11. If you have kept your eyes closed, open them. If they were open, focus your gaze on one point. You are now ready to continue your preparation or make your first astral projection attempt.

The Roots (Grounding Exercise)

Are you nervous about losing your balance and feeling unsafe after your return? Preparatory grounding can help you feel connected to the physical world, making you feel safer and balanced regardless of your journey.

Like the previous exercise, this exercise is about focusing on your physical body's sensations. The exception is that here, you will connect with the earth and allow it to draw away negative energy from you.

Instructions:

1. Stand or sit with your feet planted firmly on the ground.
2. Take a few deep breaths and feel yourself relaxing.
3. Imagine small vines suddenly sprouting from your feet and making their way into the ground. See them grow and become stronger until they look like the roots of a tree anchoring it to the ground.
4. Focus on the connection between the ground and your feet. Feel yourself anchored to the physical world. Wherever your voyage takes you, thinking of this connection will help you find your way back.
5. Let the roots grow deep, and feel yourself establishing a steady energy flow through this connection.
6. Imagine negativity traveling down through this connection and into the earth. It's replaced with the positive energy coming from the ground into your feet and body.
7. Continue with this exercise until you feel grounded and confident enough that you will be able to return safely.

Astral Projection Music

Do you like to listen to music while doing mundane tasks? If so, it may be because you find it relaxing. You are not alone. Many people like to relax with the help of music, including when preparing for astral travel. For this, you will need music that helps you to relax - for example, meditation soundtracks or any other piece with sound and rhythm you find easy to align with. Or it may be music that involves chanting or drumming, like the music shamans use when preparing to enter a deeply meditative state. Once your energy begins to connect to the frequencies of the music, you will start relaxing.

Listening to music may help you focus on astral projection.'

Instructions:

1. Create a relaxing atmosphere. Dim the lights, put on the music, and eliminate distractions like digital gadgets, pets, etc.

2. Focus on the music permeating your ears. Feel its vibrations traveling from your head to your toes. Feel yourself relaxing under its beats and tones.

3. You can combine this exercise with meditation or deep breathing. After letting yourself relax with the music, you can try meditating until you reach a hypnagogic state.

4. Or you can simply continue relaxing with music until you are ready to start your journey.

Harnessing the Power of Crystals

Crystals associated with chakra energy can be wonderful for channeling your focus. Stones linked to the crown and third eye chakras are particularly beneficial as they can help you forge the pathway to your inner wisdom. Like other crystals, these have their unique energy, which you can harness and join with your own to prepare for your journey.

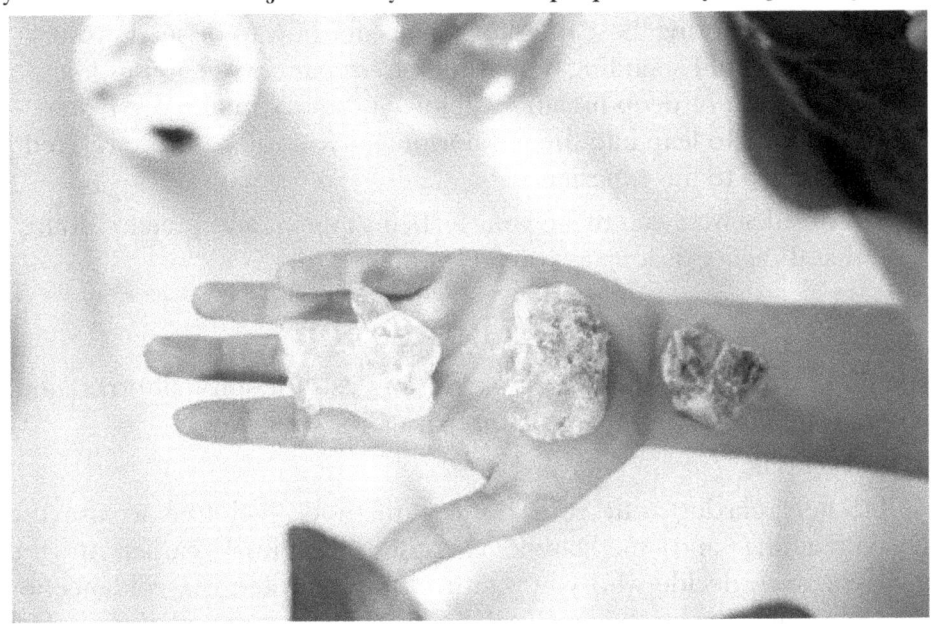

Crystals are great for tapping into chakra energy.[10]

In addition to empowerment, crystals can also protect you, making you feel safer at the beginning of your journey. Because they provide a connection to spiritual wisdom and natural energy, they can act as anchors for the spiritual path you are preparing to explore.

Let Go of Fear

Having some fear is natural when you are delving into the unknown - and astral travel is mysterious, even if you learn how to prepare for it. It is a unique experience, depending on personal choices, preferences, needs, backgrounds, thoughts, feelings, and reactions.

Paradoxically, you can never be fully relaxed (and hence, focused) until you let go of fear. Wondering how to do that? Following the instructions below:

Instructions:
1. Get comfortable and take a few deep breaths. Let your body and mind relax with each inhale and exhale.
2. Think about where your fear of astral traveling comes from. Are you nervous about taking the first step? Do you feel scared of what you may encounter on your journeys? Are you afraid that being

overly excited will get in the way of your focus?
3. After answering these questions, consider how to dissuade your fears. Would spending more time on preparatory exercises like meditation or deep breathing help? These may make you better equipped to leap into the unknown, and you will be more relaxed and open to the experience.
4. Consider what can make your fears disappear, and practice doing that. Practice as long as you feel you need to.

Ask for Protection

You do not have to be in the astral realm to ask for spiritual protection. You can do this while you are still preparing for your trip.

Instructions:
1. After relaxing with your desired method (feel free to use the breathing and meditation exercises described earlier in the chapter), decide who you want to ask for protection, guidance, or blessing. It can be any person or entity that makes you feel reassured when you think of them (an ancestor, recently deceased loved one, deity, spirit animal, etc.).
2. Then, call on the person or entity you thought of. You do not have to ask them anything. Just say their name and think of them. Let the thought of their presence envelop you with peacefulness and security.

Exit Strategy

Having an exit strategy will be like a safety net for a beginner. Once again, you just need to focus on what helps you prepare. How do you determine your exit strategy? Answer the following questions:

- What would make you feel safe when learning to separate your astral body from your physical body? Is there an action you can do to reassure yourself that you can stop when you start feeling unsafe during the process?
- Would making a quick exit be better than slowly transitioning into a separate state?
- Is there a technique that helps you kick your imagination into high gear? If so, experiment with this technique.

Intention Setting

Intention setting is another crucial preparatory step for successful astral travel. Even if you are yet to make your first journey, setting an intention for it will help you feel more confident and focused on the task at hand. Your intent will be your compass, guiding you so you will not get overwhelmed or lost.

Instructions:

1. After relaxing with one of the methods mentioned at the beginning of this chapter, think about what you want to achieve during your first attempts. For example, you can set the intention to make your first visualization fruitful, or you may set the intention to feel safe and be open about the experience.

2. If you choose the latter, take a deep breath and say:

    "I intend to start my astral journey safely and with an open mind about what I'll learn and discover."

3. Focus on your intention. Let the words permeate your mind, body, and soul. Sit with them and repeat them if necessary.

4. When you feel ready, continue with your preparatory steps like visualization, deep breathing, etc.

You can produce other intentions depending on what your goal is. As with any other subject, intention will be the way to go if you want to expand your knowledge and practical skills in astral projection. Overall, you should focus on what would help you prepare for the journey, not the journey itself – you will learn more about that in the next chapters.

Chapter 4: Induction Methods for Successful Travels

Astral Projection, or out-of-body experience (OBE), is a phenomenon in which consciousness or the astral body becomes separated from the physical body, allowing it to explore nonphysical dimensions or realms. The practice comes from the belief that the soul is not attached to the body, which allows the soul to go beyond ordinary known limits. It has been believed for centuries by many cultures, mostly associated with self-discovery and transcendence.

The out-of-body experience relies on many elements to ensure a safe and meaningful journey. The most important aspect is to balance deep physical relaxation while maintaining a heightened mental alertness. The element of being relaxed yet conscious is essential for the heavenly experience. This means the body must be free from tension while the mind stays focused and awake. This balance is what prevents practitioners from drifting into unconscious sleep and enables them to detach the astral body from its physical form. Another key element is the vibrational state, similar to a sensation of vibrations or buzzing, which is believed to signify the separation process.

When planning to practice astral projection, focused intentions play a crucial role. Using techniques such as affirmations and visualization is essential to overcoming mental barriers and navigating the astral realm effectively.

The Importance of Relaxing

Complete relaxation is a vital step for a successful astral projection experience. A calm and relaxed body can allow the practitioner to channel energy from their body into their conscious awareness. When the practitioner minimizes distraction, quietening all physical sensations, their mind can gain clarity and control to begin the OBE. Creating this balance between relaxing and maintaining consciousness ensures a seamless transition between physical and astral states.

Astral Travel Induction

Astral travel induction is when the practitioner prepares the mind and body to begin their journey beyond the physical realm. Proper preparations are required as the consciousness is separated from the body and explores other dimensions and realms. This practice relies on mental discipline, relaxation techniques, and a certain state of awareness to complete the out-of-body experience.

How to Prepare

There are many ways to complete astral travel induction. The most effective method is through breathwork. Breathwork techniques require deep, rhythmic breaths that are specifically designed to calm the nervous system and expand mental awareness. The most common breathwork technique is the 4-7-8 breathing method. This method requires the practitioner to inhale while counting to four, hold their breath for the count of seven, and exhale slowly for eight counts. The practitioner should repeat the process a few times until they reach a meditative state that can help them transition easier into the astral realm.

Breathing exercises help you focus to achieve astral travel.[11]

Some practitioners prefer the hypnogogic focus technique for astral travel induction. This method puts the practitioner between wakefulness and sleep, which offers a natural gateway for astral travel. To use this technique, practitioners lie still with their eyes closed, and as they drift closer to sleep, they observe the images and sensations that arise. This technique aims to focus on the images and sensations while resisting the urge to sleep and lose consciousness. By doing this, practitioners can depend on their experience and be able to separate their consciousness from their physical body.

"Affirmation and mental repetition" are employed in one of the methods practitioners use for astral travel induction. It relies on positive affirmations and repetitive statements to prime the mind for astral travel. Statements such as "I am safe to explore the astral realm," "I will separate from my body," or "I can perform astral travel easily" can help prep the mind, reinforce intentions, and reduce fear or doubt. By doing this, the practitioner prepares their mind for the experience they are about to have and focuses their subconscious on the goal.

Other practitioners use the energy body focus technique, which emphasizes directing awareness and attention to the subtle energy fields within the body. The method involves focusing an imagined energy ball on different body parts, starting at the toes and gradually shifting the focus to the shoulders and head. By doing this, practitioners heighten their awareness of the energetic self and enhance the feeling of detachment from the physical form.

The body awareness exercise is the last astral travel induction method practitioners use to prepare for OBE. This technique involves visualizing moving a non-physical version of your arm or leg while focusing on breathing simultaneously. This technique prepares the mind for the experience by gradually building familiarity with the sensation of gradually separating from the body.

Astral Travel and Lucid Dreaming

Lucid dreaming is the experience of being aware that you are dreaming without waking up. This state of consciousness allows individuals to actively influence their dreams, control events, and interact with the subconscious mind. Many practitioners believe it is closely linked to astral travel, as it creates a ground base for experiencing OBE. Lucid dreaming heightens the awareness and control of an individual's unconscious mind, helping them enhance their consciousness beyond the dream realm and through astral travel.

Lucid dreaming provides a conscious platform where individuals can practice separating their awareness from the dream body. After a while, they can focus on separating their consciousness from their physical body and experience the OBE. Practitioners can use lucid dreaming by visualizing themselves separating from their dream body, then stepping into a portal that leads to the astral realm, which can create a bridge between the dream state and astral projection.

Reality Checks

Reality checks are essential tools for inducing lucid dreaming and astral travel. These checks are essential as they involve questioning the nature of reality throughout the day. For example, individuals can try to push a finger through the palm of their opposite hand to sense the pressure. They can also check the time constantly or observe a certain text to see if it shifts or moves. Regularly doing these checks and making them a habit can help practitioners use them in their dreams. When they recognize that they are dreaming, individuals can gain the lucidity needed to guide their experience toward astral travel.

Using Anchors

Practitioners use anchor techniques to stabilize awareness and prevent premature waking during lucid dreaming. Anchors can include focusing on sensations such as rubbing hands together or touching objects within the dream. This helps the dreamer stabilize their consciousness, and they can use these anchors as starting points to initiate astral projection.

When practitioners combine lucid dreaming practices with reality checks and anchors, they can cultivate their awareness and gain the control they need for astral travel.

Signs You Are Close to a Projection

A few signs can occur as the body and consciousness transition into the state needed for astral projection. These signs signal the separation of the astral body from the physical body. When practitioners recognize these signals, they can be used as reassurance and guidance to remain calm and focused during the experience.

Vibrational Sensations

The most common sign individuals can experience is a vibrational sensation throughout the body. This sensation can feel like buzzing, tingling, or waves of energy moving from head to toe. They can be subtle or, for some, overwhelming. However, they are harmless and merely indicate that the energetic body is preparing to escape from the physical body. It is essential to stay relaxed and allow this sensation to intensify until you complete the OBE.

Auditory Signs

Along with vibrational sensation, sounds are often one of the signs. Some practitioners experience auditory signals, including humming, buzzing, or even high-pitched tones. Some people have reported hearing whooshing sounds or even snippets of voices or music. The sounds are not external but can be heard from shifting awareness between physical and astral states. One can deepen their experience and encourage the transition by focusing on these sounds without fear.

Visual Phenomena

When the astral body is preparing for separation, visual cues may occur even while the eyes are closed. These visual cues can be swirling lights, flashes, or geometric patterns. Some practitioners report a tunnel-like effect or a glowing portal. These visual signs indicate that the consciousness is closer to the astral realm. Individuals should observe these lights closely but without attachment to help maintain the balance of astral travel.

Floating Sensation

One of the signs that the astral body is separating is the feeling of lightness or a floating-like sensation. Practitioners claim to sense their bodies becoming weightless or as if they are being lifted. The sensation can begin with an arm or leg rising, then the whole body. The practitioner should let go and not resist the feeling as they detach their astral body.

Separation can be identified by a floating sensation.[18]

Sense of Peace

The last sign practitioners experience is a profound sense of peace and detachment. This state is natural as the practitioner is in a meditative state, and it indicates readiness for astral travel. While experiencing the last signal, individuals should remain calm and relax their minds to have a smooth and successful transition.

Practical Techniques for Astral Projection

Astral projection involves separating the astral body from the physical form, allowing individuals to explore the non-physical realms. There are a few techniques that can help practitioners perform astral travel smoothly.

The Rope Technique

The rope technique is the most common method practitioners use for astral projection. This method relies mainly on maintaining a deep state of relaxation and visualization. Here is a step-by-step guide to complete astral travel through the rope technique:

- Find a quiet, dimly lit, or dark room where you can lie down comfortably.
- Close your eyes and take a few deep breaths. Inhale slowly and deeply through your nostrils for four seconds, hold your breath for another four seconds, and exhale slowly through your

mouth for six seconds. Repeat this step until you feel completely relaxed and all tension leaves your body.

- Focus your consciousness on relaxing every muscle. Visualize each body part becoming heavy and relaxed. Start with your toes and work your way up to your head.
- Set your intention for the astral travel by repeating affirmations or mantras. This could be "I will climb the rope and transition into the astral realm." Repeat it five times to shift your focus onto the intention.
- Allow your body to feel relaxed and heavy as if it is sinking into the floor or bed. However, keep your mind alert and aware enough to resist falling asleep.
- Feel the transition as it happens. Focus your consciousness on any sensations, such as tingling, buzzing, or vibrations in your body. These can indicate that your astral body is ready to separate. When these sensations occur, relax and let them flow without fear.
- As these sensations occur, visualize a strong, thick rope hanging from above - and within reach. With your eyes closed, try to picture the rope vividly in your mind with details such as the texture, weight, and how it feels in your hands.
- When you can see the rope clearly with your mind, imagine extending your astral arms and grabbing the rope. Focus on the sensation of pulling yourself upwards until you feel your grip. You should feel the motion of your astral body as you ascend.
- Some individuals report twitching or changes in breathing. That is normal. You should maintain focus on the rope image and regulate your breathing, as these are natural signs of transition.
- When you feel the grip, pull your other astral arm and climb until you feel lightness or detachment. When you feel your astral body is completely detached, let go of the rope and allow yourself to float freely into the astral realm.

Wake-Initiated Lucid Dreaming (WILD)

Wake-initiated lucid dreaming is an astral projection technique many individuals prefer. It is the process of transitioning from being fully awake to the dream state while maintaining full awareness. You can try this method during your afternoon nap, as your body is naturally prepared to relax. You can practice when you go to bed at night, but you should ensure you are not too tired to maintain awareness, or you can try it right after 5 to 6 hours of sleep.

- The first thing you need to do is to set your intention by repeating affirmations. For example, "I will become lucid" and "I will enter my dreams fully aware." You should also ensure your room is completely quiet, with no distractions or noise. Try to clear your mind before it as well so there will be no thoughts lingering in your mind, and you can stay fully focused on your goal.
- Lie comfortably on your back on the bed or on a yoga mat with your arms and legs in a relaxed position.
- Close your eyes and take a few deep and slow breaths.
- As you relax, you may experience seeing some images or patterns in your mind. These are usually signs that you are entering the dream state.
- Focus on these images and begin to direct them as they become clearer. You can do so by visualizing a detailed picture. Visualize the sensation, colors, and sounds.
- As the dream becomes clearer, repeat your affirmations and remind yourself that you are dreaming.
- The next step is to transition from the lucid dream to the astral realm by redirecting your awareness towards your astral body. Visualize yourself walking away from the dream state and into the astral realm.

Body Displacement

The body displacement method focuses on the gradual detachment of the astral body. It is about separating each part slowly until you reach full separation.

- Begin the technique with a deep breathing exercise to calm your physical body. At the same time, state your intention and repeat your affirmations.
- Close your eyes and keep your awareness focused on your astral hand. Visualize yourself lifting it an inch above your physical hand.

- Once you feel your astral hand moving, redirect your focus to another part, for example, your astral feet or the other astral arm. Picture yourself lifting it slightly above the physical body and repeat the process until your whole body feels weightless or lifted.
- Picture your whole astral body lifting gently from your physical form.

Magnet Pull Technique

The magnet pull technique relies mainly on the power of visualization to perform astral projection. It involves picturing a magnetic force pulling your astral body away from your physical one.

- Lie down on a comfortable surface and start with deep, slow breaths to relax your body. Keep your body relaxed and comfortable, and let your mind become quiet and clear from thoughts.
- Set your intentions and repeat your mental affirmations.
- Visualize a magnetic force somewhere above you and imagine a soft force pulling you toward it like different poles of magnets attracting each other.
- Keep your focus on the sensation of being pulled or drawn upward toward the magnet.
- You may begin to feel tingling, a subtle shift in your body, or a feeling of lightness, which means that the detachment is happening.
- Let the magnet easily pull you upward and let go of any resistance.
- As you feel the separation from your physical body, maintain your focus on the magnetic pull, as it can help keep your awareness focused on the transition and prevent distractions, thoughts, or fears.

Energy Surge Method

Another common method that practitioners use is the energy surge method. It uses the flow of energy throughout the body to assist in the astral projection experience.

- Start by lying in a quiet, comfortable place without distractions or noise. Close your eyes and take deep rhythmic breaths to relax your body and clear your thoughts. With each exhale, imagine you are releasing all tension from your body.
- While you are breathing, set your intention and mentally repeat your affirmations. You can say, "I am allowing the energy to rise through my body," "I am safe while separating from my physical body," or anything along those lines.
- Once you say your affirmations a few times, visualize a wave of energy starting from your toes and flowing through your body to your head. Picture the warm energy moving throughout your body, and as you breathe in, see it rise from your feet to your head.
- When you feel a tingling or a buzzing sensation, it means that the energy is starting to intensify. At this point, visualize the energy rising in your body. Wait until you feel the energy is at its peak. It may feel like a surge of power or a wave of euphoria. This means your astral body is aligning with the energy flow.
- Visualize yourself releasing the energy, and as you are doing so, feel your astral body lifting from the physical body. Allow yourself to flow into the astral realm smoothly by maintaining focus on the energy.

Floating Visualziation

Floating visualization is another method practitioners use for astral travel. It relies on imagining yourself floating in water or air and enhancing the sensation of being weightless.

- Relax your body completely. You could lie down on your back or in any other comfortable and relaxed position. Close your eyes and choose a breathing technique that helps relax your body completely and bring clarity to your mind. Repeat breathing until your mind is free of thoughts, distractions, or fear. Focus mainly on your breathing and on relaxing your body.
- Once your mind is clear, imagine yourself floating in a body of water or the air. To do that, picture yourself weightless, as if you were floating on water, and picture that no gravity is pulling you.

- The feeling of weightlessness is the key to this method, so maintain your focus on this visualization and how it feels to be free from any pressure or tension. Keep all your awareness on this sensation and let it intensify with every breath.
- To keep your awareness of this feeling, picture each body part as weightless.
- Feeling a sense of lightness or detachment means your astral body is in the separation process. Embrace this feeling and let your astral body float freely while your physical body is completely relaxed.

Sound Frequency

Many individuals use sound frequency for astral projection and consider it one of the best tools for OBE. This method relies on binaural beats, humming, or other sounds that help program your consciousness and prepare it for astral travel.

- Practitioners use many sound frequencies for astral travel, which is why selecting an audio that resonates with you is essential. It could be humming sounds, beats designed in certain frequencies, or meditation sounds. Usually, the sound should contain binaural beats, which is a sound played in two slightly different frequencies in each ear. The brain can pick up on these frequencies and it can synchronize brainwave patterns. Like any other technique, begin by preparing your environment. Choose a quiet place with no distractions or noise.
- Find good quality headphones that fit your ears without irritating you and don't move or fall off while sleeping. You should also adjust the volume to a comfortable level, not too low so you will not drift into sleep, and not too loud so it does not bother you and prevent you from astral travel.
- Once you find the right headphones and prepare your environment, lie down in any comfortable position and close your eyes. Start with deep and slow breaths and keep all your focus on your breathing patterns. With each breath, picture all the tension leaving your body.
- Once the sound begins, shift all your focus from your breath to the sound and let it fill your awareness. Breathe slowly and let

the sound synchronize with your mind and body.

- As your mind is focusing on the sound, let your body relax and drift more with every breath.
- When you begin to feel the sensation of lightness or detachment, continue to listen to the sound and maintain your focus on it. When the sound becomes very noticeable, and you feel it is completely in sync with your body, let it guide you to the astral realm and begin to detach your astral body from the physical one.

Developing Anchoring Technique

Anchoring techniques are ways that help practitioners establish mental markers that help them recognize whether they are awake, in a dream state, or in the astral realm. The anchor can be a physical object, sound, a person's face, or a person's voice. The purpose of this technique is for the practitioner to know they are in the dream state.

Before performing your astral travel, you should have an anchor that serves as a signal to help you realize when you are dreaming or in an astral state.

Start by selecting the item. Choose anything you are familiar with and see in your daily life. It could be an object you used to have, a person's face, or the sound of the waves. Once you select the anchor, try to take a few moments throughout your day to recognize these anchors. For example, if you choose the sound of waves and you are walking by the beach, remind yourself that this sound could appear in a dream state.

Doing this every day can help increase your awareness and your concentration skills. The more you practice with your anchors, the more reliable they become. Good anchors can help you distinguish between the dream and astral state, and you can maintain awareness and control throughout your experience.

Chapter 5: Navigating the Astral Plane

Once you have achieved separation from your physical body and have entered the astral realm, you will need to know how to navigate it safely and effectively. This chapter will provide tips and techniques to build your awareness and learn how to confidently perform astral travel.

The Astral Planes

You may wonder how to recognize the astral state or feeling of being in the astral body. There are several signs your spirit has now shifted into astral mode. The first one will be the sensation of movement. It is very much like when you sit in a car, and it starts to move. Some people have a short moment of feeling unable to move right before this.

Along with the movement, you may also feel a buzzing sensation washing over your body due to the change in vibrations around you. You may feel a slight pressure on your chest, followed by a feeling of lightness.

There are several sensations you will feel with projecting into the astral plane.[18]

Next, you will likely see lights and colors flash in front of your eyes and suddenly realize you can fly or float. You may be able to look down on your body and see vibrant lights dancing around it, too.

After the visual experiences, you may start hearing foreign sounds and noises (things that do not come from your physical environment). This can be a little disorienting, but you will get used to it.

You will have a heightened sense of clarity once you get through the initial unusual experiences. You will feel very aware of yourself and your surroundings – perhaps even more than your physical body.

Along with this initial shift of physician sensations, you will experience some emotional ups and downs. First (especially during the initial attempts), you will feel fear. This is normal but can hinder you from moving along with your journey and push you back into your physical body.

If the separation is quick, this can cause even more fear, and so can the sensation of sudden movement. Once you realize that you can move freely and are in control, you can overcome this fear (with practice). Over time, you will learn that fear is fuel, not an opponent.

Knowing what you may encounter can also dissuade your fears. The astral plane is a multifaceted environment consisting of the lower (including the near-earth plane), middle, and higher planes. The near-earth plane is closest to physical reality, and here, you might see familiar faces, objects, and environments. However, you will already experience the effects of the higher vibrations. Some prefer to linger in the near-earth plane and start exploring the astral realm here without stepping into the other planes. This and the other lower planes present an excellent opportunity to develop your navigation and communication skills. You may encounter other astral travelers, deceased loved ones, and spiritual beings who can offer guidance on how to master projection.

The middle realms offer much more freedom and inspire spiritual learning. Void of limitations like physical needs and desires (for example, you may notice that you do not feel hungry, thirsty, or tired no matter how long you wander across these realms) or issues that cause insecurities and conflicts. Yet, you may see it as the reflection of the physical world, perhaps enhanced by your perception of your surroundings. For example, if you see something in a positive light, you may notice rainbows and pops of vivid colors appearing around objects, people, and animals. The beings you will encounter here will often offer their help, sending silent messages to asked and unasked questions. They can provide ideas, inspiration, and dream symbols and help you manifest whatever intention resonates with you. Many travel here to heal from emotional and spiritual wounds (whether theirs or ancestral ones). With practice, you may even be able to glimpse into future and past events. Keep in mind that these, too, will be colored by your perception, so if you see something that is beyond your comprehension, you should only focus on the message you can extract from the experience.

The higher planes are often described as purely otherworldly, containing nothing you may find in the real world. You can only reach them after extensive practice and developing skills like trusting your intuition. The beings you will encounter here are those who have achieved the highest level of spirituality. Their role is to inspire you to grow and become fully aware of the world's interconnectedness. They can help you see how every choice you make in the physical world impacts all the other realms – and guide you as you explore all these effects in the other realms. As time passes differently in these planes, they're the perfect place for healing – spiritual, emotional, and physical. Exploring them can expand your perception of everything in life, freeing you of biases, societal stigmas, and insecurities. Everything you see here looks distorted because it is symbolic, and just like the middle planes, the higher planes offer the benefit of raising your awareness and opening up your consciousness to everything positive.

As you move from the lower planes and up to the higher ones, you slowly transition from a deep connection to the physical world to a faraway reality where only the need to learn and explore exists. From the worries of the physical world, you step into a reality where all your dreams, hopes, and desires can come to life. All you need to make this happen is to learn to navigate the astral planes. How? For starters, by learning how to move in them.

Intent-Based Movement

In the astral realm, everything works through imagination and intent. You can visualize, do, and experience everything you want using these. When you intend to move in a certain way, you are signaling your astral body to do just that – and the stronger the intent is, the easier it will be to do it.

Instructions:

1. For example, if you visualize a quest, like getting to a door across the room, and focus on arriving there in the astral state, you will be able to do it.
2. Do not think about the steps, how far you need to go, or anything similar as you would in the physical world. Just say to yourself, "I intend to get to that door." or "I am getting to the door."
3. Then, see yourself standing at the door. Practice until you can state your intention with belief and start moving with intent.

Floating or Flying

Traveling while floating or flying is much easier than traversing any distance in the physical world, but you must still use plenty of willpower and practice diligently. Always set a target in your mind and use a technique that ensures you will succeed. Here is a great example of how to do it:

Instructions:

1. When the pressure of getting into the astral state eases, focus on feeling weightless. Feel yourself becoming lighter and lighter.
2. Now, picture yourself doing a movement that comes naturally. It can be floating, flying, lingering, and moving at any speed you feel comfortable with.

3. Find a distant point you want to reach. This can be a larger landmark you can see from far away.
4. Let whatever motion feels natural to you propel you forward.
5. Imagine yourself moving toward the chosen point, steered only by the desire to get there.

Additional Practical Tips for Moving

When you begin flying or floating, you may have the natural instinct to go upward. This is likely due to recent separation and entering the astral state, wherein your astral body is lifted away from your physical body. If this happens, just steer your mind (you travel in the direction that is in your mind) toward a focal point or destination.

Use your energy body to your advantage. Try practicing energy manipulation throughout your energy body, like you would through your physical body. Visualize your aura and channel your energy toward your intent to move in a way you want to.

You may also find it useful to establish an anchor point during your first attempts. There could be more than one, as these could make maneuvering easier initially. As you travel, notice and become aware of landmarks that pop into your attention. Memorize them, and if you have trouble navigating the journey back or are not sure where to go next, you can always return to your anchor points to reorient yourself.

If you come across any entity, approach them slowly. What is your gut telling you about them? Do they seem trustworthy? If so, you should move slightly closer but only slowly. Stop at a comfortable distance where you can establish communication. For example, stand far enough so you can look into their eyes but not so far as to make them guess your intention. Likewise, when you get close enough to see their eyes, you can start communicating by sending them thoughts of greeting without scaring them.

Some practitioners also find it useful to have a mantra or phrase they can repeat to anchor their movements. For example, you can repeat to yourself:

"I can fly wherever I want."

"I'm floating high or low, wherever my mind takes me now."

"I can move freely. Nothing is limiting me but my mind."

If you find yourself drifting in a direction you do not want to go, channel your mind back to the phrase, and you will be back on track soon.

Another option is to count while traveling. This can help you pace your journeys and act as an anchor for repeated visits.

Potential Obstacles and Hazards

During and immediately after separation, you may encounter obstacles like being too excited or overly analytical. Much like fear, being too excited can slam you back into your physical body, ending your journey before it begins. To prevent this, try to practice controlling your emotions.

It is natural to feel excited about finally stepping onto the astral planes. It can inspire you to let go of the fear and start exploring deeper. However, when you learn how to calm yourself after separation, your journey will become much more enjoyable, not to mention productive. You can do this by doing a quick meditation or breathing exercise. For the latter, simply take slow, deep breaths until your heart stops hammering in your chest and your breathing slows down naturally. You should be able to control your mind and not be distracted by your excitement. Maintain calm throughout your journey and repeat the deep breathing session if you feel yourself getting over-excited again.

Stopping and overanalyzing everything you see will also hinder your success. While highly symbolic, not everything you experience in the astral realm has a hidden or profound meaning. Most of it is just a reflection of your mind, specifically your psyche.

Astral Entities

The beings you may encounter during astral projection will also likely reflect your imagination – but do not be surprised if you meet entities with distinct characteristics.

Who are these beings? They can be spirit guides, deceased loved ones, negative entities, or other astral travelers like yourself. Spirit guides are loving and helpful and want to connect to you to guide you on your journeys. They can also encourage your spiritual growth by feeding you thoughts of wisdom or sending you signs to uncover spiritual knowledge.

By contrast, negative entities are likely to try to deceive you or hinder your journey. Unlike the previous group, which often has vibrant energy, the negative beings are dark and can make you feel uneasy. Fortunately, you will be far less likely to encounter a negative being than a positive one. Why? As a general rule of thumb, in the astral world, positivity attracts positivity. Unless your vibrations are very low and you have lots of negativity in yourself, you will be projecting to a realm where negative entities do not hang around.

Deceased loved ones can be the spirits of people you have recently lost or ancestors who lived much before your time. They, too, may offer guidance and wisdom and communicate through signs and emotions. They may make you experience sensations, receive intuitive messages, or hear a familiar voice telling you about the next steps you should take on your journey. Some may look human, while others have translucent forms (as you will only see their spirits). Like spirit guides, ancestral spirits will only approach you out of curiosity and without malicious intent.

A unique form of spirit guide you may encounter on your travels is the elemental spirit. As guardians of the natural realm, elementals are connected to specific elements and have no physical bodies. They communicate through emotions, by manipulating energy and sending it your way, or by causing physical sensations you must interpret to decipher their message. They, too, are generally benevolent and wish to guide you on your journey.

Other astral travelers are spiritual seekers with different levels of experience. Some can teach you, but others will want to be left alone because they do not know what to expect from a fellow traveler.

So, how do you interact with these different entities? In the beginning, you may want to simply stick to simple observation. Do not rush to engage them if you feel that the being in front of you is benevolent or not. If you know you will want to make contact but are not sure how to do that, ask for some guidance (it does not have to be specific. You can simply address your spirit guides even if you have not met them before) on how to communicate. They may reach out to you once you enter the astral realm and approach you themselves.

It is crucial to set clear boundaries, and not just for yourself. The other beings will also feel more secure if you build your relationship with mutual trust and respect. Maintain a grounded mindset to avoid getting carried away with excitement when meeting a helpful being. Likewise, with clear boundaries in place, you will be more likely to repel unwanted energies or entities that want to tag along without your permission.

Defense Within a Sphere

While it can be a wonderful experience, astral traveling has risks. There might be a time when you need to defend yourself from unwanted energies or entities. Here is a visualization method that can help you prepare for defense should you encounter something that makes you feel threatened.

Instructions:
1. Take several deep, calming breaths. Breathe until you begin to feel relaxed and your mind clears.
2. Now, visualize a bright energy sphere descending from above you and enveloping your astral body from all sides. Feel its protective warmth.
3. Focus on making it very visible and strong so nothing can penetrate it.
4. Then, channel positive, empowering thoughts like:

    "I'm more powerful than any being that may try to harm me."

    "I'm strong enough to repel any negativity that presents itself to me."

    "Nothing can harm me within this bubble."
5. Focusing on these thoughts, feel the positive energy swell within you. Direct it outward toward the sphere.
6. Let the positive energy infuse your protective bubble.
7. Now, visualize it repelling negativity.
8. Continue your travel, reassured with confidence that nothing will be able to harm you now.

For the best results, practice this while preparing for your journey. You can incorporate it into a preparatory meditation or use it as a standalone exercise. This will be helpful if you lack confidence in your skills or fear that you will be harmed while traveling. It will raise vibrations and empower your intention for safe, confident astral travel. If you use it as a preparatory exercise, you can start by imagining white light surrounding your body and claiming you before attempting the separation.

You could alternatively do the visualization when encountering a harmful entity. It's best to avoid direct confrontation and to simply focus on letting your energy shield defend you. Even if you are not afraid and your vibrations are high enough to connect with the astral realm easily, confronting malevolent beings will only infuse you with negativity.

Handling Negative Energy or Entities

What do you do when encountering an unpleasant entity or negative energy from an unknown source? You remain calm, assert your intent to defend yourself, and continue your journey in peace.

Instructions:

1. Visualize a protective sphere around you.
2. State your intention – try to address the entity directly. For example, you can say: "You have no power here."
3. If you have made connections with a spirit guide before, ask for their help.
4. Take deep breaths to remain calm and maintain a positive attitude.
5. See the protective sphere around you glowing brightly and the negative entity turning away. Show the entities your power, and do not let them intimidate you.
6. Keep focusing on maintaining the protective bubble around you until the entire leaves.

Visualization to Dissolve Negative Energies

Remember, your imagination is your most formidable power in the astral world. Using it, you can repel or dissolve any energy threatening or hindering you on your journey.

Instructions:

1. Similar to the previous method, imagine being surrounded by an orb of warm light full of loving positivity.
2. When creating the orb in your mind, consider replacing negativity with positivity. What sort of negative energy are you getting from the entity? What can you use to counter them?
3. Infuse your shield with positivity, love, and compassion. Then, channel these feelings toward the entity. After all, the best way to fight dark is to attack it with light. Love and compassion will help dissolve them so they stop bothering you.

4. If you have trouble channeling positivity toward a negative entity or energy, remember they are you. They are the result of your negative perception. You may be hesitant to send love and compassion to them, but you can send them to yourself.

Exiting the Astral Plane

Signs You Are Ready to Come Back

How do you know you are ready to return from the astral plane? You do that by relying on your intuition. You will feel that you have learned what you needed and can now return to ponder on the wisdom.

You may become tired (interactions within the astral realm can be exhausting, especially for beginners) physically and mentally. Even if you have not encountered anything negative, you may still feel you have had enough.

Re-entering Your Physical Body

With a little bit of practice, you can also set up a safety line that pulls you back when you need to re-enter your physical body.

Instructions:

1. Before you separate, visualize a cord connecting your astral and physical bodies.
2. When you have finished your exploration and are ready to return, set your intention on reuniting with your physical body.
3. Grab the rope, and counting from one to ten, pull yourself gently back to the physical realm, merging your astral being with your body.
4. Then, focus on your physical sensations. Where does your body connect to the surface on which it sits, stands, and lies? What do you feel in your fingers? How about your chest and shoulders?
5. You may feel a buzzing sensation as your energy re-enters and flows through your body.
6. Then, start moving your body slowly. Do not rush. However long the session lasted, it may have felt like hours for you (remember, time flows differently in the other realms). Let your breathing return to its natural rhythms, and your energy reinforce your body from the inside out.

In some cases, you may experience an abrupt return. This can happen even if you have initiated the reentry, but it is more likely when you encounter something that frightens or overwhelms you. In any case, try to remain calm and breathe deeply. Ground yourself with the root exercise you used to prepare and see where things went wrong.

Astral Travel Journaling

Journaling is a wonderful way to record your experience and gain a learning tool to improve your projection attempts. By writing down what you saw, learned, or what happened to you, you can gain a deeper insight into how astral projection works, what you find beneficial, what you do not find useful, and what can give you the control you need for successful projections.

Astral travel journaling is a wonderful way to assess your process.[14]

Making a journal entry as soon as you have reunited with your physical body is a good idea. It is like taking notes right after a class while everything is fresh in your mind. When doing this:

- Describe your experience in detail
- Note any sensory changes you had (did anything feel different)
- Describe your environment

- Write down what you did – how did you move and navigate your journey?
- Talk about your interactions
- Describe your feelings
- Write down what you have learned from the experience.

Based on the experience you have recorded in your journal, you can outline an action plan for an improved projection. For example, if you had trouble moving or think it could have gone more smoothly, you can refine your technique. Did you use anchor points? Did you channel your energy? Did something hinder your awareness? Answering these questions will help you find a better way to move around on the astral plane.

Or, if you find your interactions wherever you went were unsatisfactory (for example, you have not learned anything from them), find another destination. You may encounter more helpful beings or signs to unearth spiritual wisdom elsewhere.

Were you overwhelmed by intense feelings? If so, try finding a technique to help you regain calm next time. It does not matter how many times you fail to conquer these emotions. What matters is that you continue practicing.

Did you have trouble completing your separation, or were you pushed back into your physical body right after entering the ancestral planes? It can be frustrating, but the answer is, once again, that you need more practice. What pushes you back? Is it fear, insecurity, lack of confidence, excitement, lack of perspective and openness, or something else? Whatever it is, develop a plan to conquer it and raise your awareness to fully experience what the astral planes offer. For example, the lack of perspective may cause you to fail in imagining life and your surroundings in the astral world. Working on a more inspiring visualization technique may help you create any image you want for a successful trip.

Chapter 6: Healing Through the Astral

An astral realm is a place filled with energy and consciousness, representing a bridge between the physical world and higher spiritual dimensions. This realm is a vibrational space where the energy flows freely without restrictions, and the consciousness expands beyond the physical form. It is a fluid, dynamic space, making it a good space for addressing imbalances in the physical and emotional realms. Because it operates on frequencies different from those of the physical world, it is the ideal environment for healing and transformation.

An astral realm is filled with energy and consciousness.[15]

That said, it is essential to note that the astral realm energy does not follow the same rules as the physical world as it constantly shifts, moves in waves, and interacts with the energy individuals radiate in the physical and astral realms. In the physical and emotional realms, imbalances occur and cause disturbance within an individual's energy system such as the chakras and auras of humans. The problem with these disturbances is that they can manifest in physical illness, emotional distress, or even mental disorders. However, with the heightened energetic frequency, the astral realm can become a space for individuals to address these issues on a deep and vibrational level.

A Powerful Space for Healing

The astral realm is a direct extension of the physical world and can serve as a mirror to the imbalance that happens to the physical body. When individuals enter the astral realm, their consciousness and energy interact with the vibrational frequencies of this dimension, making it easier for the astral plane to heal and help realign people's energy and balance it out again. The realignment can take many forms and shapes. It could happen through energetic healing, aligning and healing the energy of this individual, or can heal through soul retrieval or even emotional purging. All of these heal the person, align their soul, and balance their emotions. When the practitioner is healed in the astral plane, and their energy flows in harmony, the physical and emotional self aligns and becomes in balance again, which means that it starts to help the person and can manifest back into the physical world.

Practitioners believe that the key element of astral healing lies in the interaction with consciousness itself. The astral plan is an environment where the mind and spirit can be freed of all the limitations of the material world. This transition allows individuals to become more deeply aware of their true selves.

As astral travel can expand consciousness, practitioners use it to access and release past traumas, emotional blockages, negative thought patterns, and negative energy stored in their physical bodies for years.

The astral realm offers the opportunity to cleanse and purify energy. That is mainly because this dimension is filled with vibrations that can help clear negative energy from the body's subtle systems and enhance a person's overall well-being. When the consciousness expands in the astral plane, and individuals can increase their awareness, they can access forgotten and suppressed memories and unresolved emotions, helping them identify what is causing the negative thoughts and healing them.

Astral healing is a practice that focuses on addressing an individual's deep-seated energetic blockage and unprocessed traumas, especially those that the individual was not able to access through physical and emotional means in the material world. This healing process happens because the dimension of the astral realm provides a space where one can interact freely with energy without limitations, allowing them to confront and heal suppressed emotions and issues that may not have existed as it was buried deep in their subconscious mind.

The ability to heal in the astral realm can allow practitioners to access and release energetic blockages that have accumulated throughout their lives. These blockages are usually the result of deep-rooted psychological issues and unresolved traumas that are trapped within the body's energy systems.

When individuals experience trauma, stress, or negative emotions and thought patterns, they are rarely released from the mind or from the body, which causes the body to store and hold on to it, leading to physical and emotional imbalances. However, in the astral realm, individuals can interact with their energy field to promote the release and healing of these blockages and facilitate healing on another deeper level.

Astral Realm Healing Functions

The astral realm is an energetic space that goes beyond time and space as known to humans and the material world. It offers a unique healing environment that people cannot access or achieve with traditional healing methods. Practitioners in the astral plane can reshape and rebalance energy in a way they cannot do in the physical world. For example, when a person experiences trauma, it can be stored in the body's cells and energy centers for years. However, with astral travel, they can have access to it and have the ability to release it through astral healing practices.

In the physical world, these traumas are stored in the subconscious, and they manifest in different physical and emotional forms that are hard to access with traditional therapy methods. In the material world, feelings such as fear, anger, or grief can be difficult to process and heal, especially if the cause is buried deep in the subconscious mind. Not having an outlet for these emotions in day-to-day life can create other illnesses, pain, and emotional imbalances. However, in the astral realm, these emotions can be confronted and healed in a shorter time than they would with traditional therapeutic methods. When this happens, the body's energy systems reset and return to a more balanced and harmonious state, which can manifest positively in the physical realm. For example, individuals who suffer from chronic illness and are unable to diagnose or treat it because they are unable to understand the root cause can access and heal it through the astral realm and reset the imbalance that happened.

Some practitioners believe that astral healing works on the energetic and emotional level and can sometimes indirectly affect the physical body. As astral healing repairs the energy in a way, it can improve physical health. Some illnesses, such as stress, anxiety, and unresolved trauma, can manifest themselves in the body, causing digestive issues, stiffness in the body, or other physical problems. When these individuals try astral healing and access the root of their illness, they also heal their physical bodies.

Preparing for Astral Healing

Preparing for it is a crucial step when you plan on practicing astral healing. It requires mental focus, emotional readiness, and energetic alignment. You are preparing yourself and the environment around you, as you should feel comfortable internally and externally for a successful healing experience.

Setting the Intention

The first step to preparing for astral healing is to set clear intentions for your experience. Setting an intention is central to all astral travel and healing practices, so this one should not be any different.

Take a moment for yourself to reflect on the purpose of why you are performing astral healing. Ask yourself what areas you want to focus on or what problems you wish to release. It could be anything from emotional trauma and energy imbalances to physical discomfort. However, your intention should be specific, clear, and positive, and to do that, you can start by writing it down and then saying it out loud to set the intention. By setting your intention, you redirect your consciousness during your astral travel and align your energy to receive healing.

Creating a Safe Space

Before you begin astral travel, clearing your mind and being emotionally calm is essential for a smooth experience. Create a peaceful environment before you start your journey. Dim the lights and stay in a quiet and comfortable place. Once you lay comfortable, begin to calm your mind to access deeper layers of consciousness. By clearing your mind and calming your thoughts completely, you can stay centered and focused during the healing process without distractions or fear. You can engage yourself in mindfulness practices to clear your thoughts. This can include deep breathing, meditation, visualization, or any practice that helps create a calm mental space. Let your thoughts flow in and out without any attachments and if you feel your mind starts to wander, guide it back by focusing on your breath and repeating the technique you chose earlier.

Create a safe and peaceful space before you begin.[16]

Some people prefer to visualize a serene space like a beach or a forest and picture themselves walking there, breathing in the natural surroundings as they allow their body and mind to relax.

Grounding Techniques

While it is essential to calm your mind before starting astral healing, grounding yourself to maintain a strong connection with your physical body while moving to the astral realm is important. As mentioned, astral travel requires balancing detaching from your physical body and maintaining a connection with it. Grounding helps prevent feelings of fear, disorientation, or becoming lost during the experience, ensuring a safe and stable experience.

To ground yourself, you can sit or lie comfortably, close your eyes, and take a few deep breaths. Start visualizing roots extending from your feet and reaching deep into the earth. Picture these roots as tough and solid and can hold your physical body during the astral experience. Start imagining the energy from the roots flowing upwards through your body, take a deep breath, and with every breath, imagine the energy fills you with a sense of stability and safety. With each exhale, picture yourself releasing any tension or stress from your body. Repeat the process until you feel safe and ready to move on to the next step.

Chakra Cleansing and Activation

Chakras are the energy centers in the physical body, and aligning them before starting your astral healing can play a significant role in your experience. When the chakras are blocked or imbalanced, they could impact your ability to access the astral plane and can disrupt the whole process.

To prepare for astral projection, cleanse and activate the chakras for a smooth transition. Start your cleansing process by focusing on each of the seven main chakras. Work your way up to the crown chakra on the crown of your head from the root chakra at the base of your spine. To start the cleansing process, visualize each one with its own color. For example, the root chakra could be red, the sacral chakra orange, the solar plexus yellow, and so on. As you picture the color for each chakra, visualize them moving in circles smoothly and brightly without any blocked energy. You can use a cleansing sound or a healing mantra with different frequencies so each can be cleansed thoroughly from negative energy.

Balancing Energy Through Breathwork

Breathing is a powerful tool in balancing and harmonizing the energy within your body to prepare for astral travel. While some breathwork to clear your mind is essential at the beginning of the process, conscious breathwork can also prepare your body and energy field for the journey. One of the most used techniques by practitioners is the box breathing method. It works by inhaling deeply for four seconds, holding your breath for four seconds, exhaling for another four seconds, holding your breath again for four seconds then exhaling for four seconds.

This method regulates the energy flow throughout your body and brings the mind into a focused yet relaxed state, which is needed to prepare the mind and body for astral travel.

Energy Alignment Through Visualization

After grounding yourself, cleansing your chakras, and clearing your mind from negative thoughts, the next step is aligning your energy to prepare it for astral healing. You can align your energy by visualizing yourself surrounded by an energy field similar to a protective aura. Imagine this energy field glowing with pure healing light, slowly expanding around you and creating a shield. Visualize this shield as strong, as it acts as a safeguard during your astral journey and cannot be impacted by any negative energy.

Preparing your environment, clearing your thoughts, cleansing your chakras, and balancing your body energy before astral healing are essential steps that prepare your mind and body for this experience and allow a smooth and easy transition. Once you have prepared yourself, it is time to move to the practical exercise that can lead you to astral healing.

Practical Exercises

Several astral healing methods are used for different types of imbalances and problems. Choose the method you most resonate with and believe will help you heal from your traumas and suppressed emotions.

Releasing Energetic Blockages

For this practice, take a deep breath and focus on it. With each breath visualize a ray of light entering your body and filling every part with warmth and peace, and with every exhale, visualize yourself releasing all the negativity and heaviness that your body may be holding onto within you. Imagine yourself transitioning out of your body, and the light frees your astral body from the physical one. Visualize your astral body glowing as it is ascending.

The next step is to focus your attention on the energy in your astral form. Start to visualize your entire astral body covered in gold or a bright stream of light. Shift your focus to every part of your astral body, and try to sense any part that feels different, heavy, dark, or blocked. You can sense when a certain part feels different from others, or you may sense an energetic disruption. However, it is essential to trust your intuition as you are identifying these blocked parts. With each breath you take, visualize the light flowing through these dark parts and transforming them into a pure golden light like the rest of your astral body. Continue doing so with each step while maintaining steady and deep breaths. You can also say some affirmations to yourself that help ease the process and show your intentions.

Remember that these blockages were formed in a matter of years, and it may take a few moments to release them all. Keep your breath steady, and imagine the light getting brighter with every breath you take. With each inhale, the light grows brighter. With each exhale, the negative emotions and limiting beliefs that no longer serve you are being released.

Healing Past Versions

If you are looking for a method to heal a past version of yourself, this is the one. This method focuses on meeting a younger version of yourself in the astral realm and offering the love and healing it needs to release emotional wounds and traumas from the past.

To start this technique, start with meditation to ensure that you are in a deeply relaxed state. Do all the grounding and breathwork techniques you learned earlier to put your mind in a calm and peaceful state, and then start the transition. Start by imagining your astral form lifting from your physical one, and it begins to float freely in a peaceful space. In this space, visualize a pathway opening before you, and your astral body is walking or floating toward this path.

As you walk down the path, trust that you will find the younger version of yourself that needs healing the most. Think of the child, teenager, or young adult of yourself who has been through a time of emotional pain or some sort of difficulty. As you walk this pathway, you find your younger self. Observe this version of you, and pay attention to their energy, expression, and needs without criticizing or judging. Allow yourself to open up to your younger self with love and compassion. Slowly approach and reassure them they are safe, loved, and protected. Say comforting words such as "You are loved" or "You are safe," and picture yourself embracing your younger self and wrapping them in a warm, protective light. Visualize yourself healing them with the light flowing from your astral form to theirs. Continue to imagine the light surrounding them, infusing them with your healing energy. Picture this light as energy healing all sadness, fear, or anger your younger self is holding. If you want to, you can speak words of affirmation and forgiveness to this younger version to reassure them that it is okay to release all the negative emotions.

Spend as much time as needed with your younger version, offering love, support, and healing. When you leave, thank them for their time, and the lessons they brought to you, and acknowledge and thank the healing you both received. After that, slowly walk back down the path you came from to return to your present self.

Chakra Cleansing in the Astral Realm

Cleansing chakras is important to balance energy and create a healthy energy field. Individuals can cleanse their chakras to clear blockages and create and maintain balance.

To cleanse your chakras in the astral realm, start by relaxing your body and clearing your mind. You can do some breathwork, meditation, or any exercise that helps you relax. Picture your astral form floating freely. When your astral body separates from your physical form, start directing all your focus on the base of your spine, the root chakra. Visualize this chakra glowing with a specific color, such as red, and that it is pulsing with energy and spinning smoothly. Focus on it and imagine the red light is growing brighter and stronger as you breathe slowly and deeply. Feel the energy from this chakra expanding and radiating a sense of stability and security that keeps growing and growing. Visualize all the negative energy and blockages clearing from your root chakra until you feel the red energy flowing freely throughout your astral body.

Once you feel it is healed, move to the next chakra in your lower abdomen and repeat the process. Continue the process on each one until you reach the third eye chakra and visualize all of them free from negativity and their energy glowing and flowing throughout your body.

Creating Astral Sacred Spaces

Creating a sacred and serene space within the astral realm can heal your energy and restore balance. It is a place where your astral form can go when you need to clear your mind, balance your energy, and heal from any problem. As with previous practices, you should prepare your physical body and clear your mind completely before you begin astral travel. Follow the same steps as you are about to astral travel, but when you begin to detach from your physical body, imagine a safe and secure path ahead of you that leads to a sacred space that feels comfortable, safe, and restorative. This sacred space can be anything that resonates with you and makes you feel healed. It could be a temple, a peaceful garden, a cave, or an underwater space. Anything that feels safe for you can be this sacred space. Let your intuition and mind lead the way and create this space for you.

The sacred space should be somewhere where the energy around you feels soothing and calm, without distractions, negativity, or judgment. As you arrive at this space, let your astral body sit or lie comfortably. This could be on the ground, a comfortable chair, or a bed. When you sit comfortably, take a deep breath and visualize this place's energy surrounding you. Imagine the warm, loving, and safe energy embracing you and allowing you to let go of all negativity.

You can visualize a stream of light entering your body and flowing all over your body from head to toe. As the light moves throughout your astral body, it clears any negative emotions, tensions, or blockages. You may feel this light fading in certain body parts, or it is not as strong as others. It means that these parts need the most care and attention. When you feel these parts, let the light flow over and over and heal it as it moves until it releases any heavy emotions and brings peace to you. Repeat the process as many times as needed until you feel this warm light is filling your whole body and you feel free from any negativity and completely relaxed.

When you feel completely healed, slowly walk down the path you came from and, at the same time, bring your awareness back to the present moment. As you walk down the path back to your physical body, know that the healing you received will continue to be with you as you return.

Releasing Emotional Energy Attachments

Emotional attachments are energetic connections that are created between individuals. Some have them from past relationships, negative experiences, family members, or others. These connections can often cause emotional distress and drain your energy, preventing you from fully moving forward with your life.

In the astral realm, you can identify and release these connections and emotional attachments and free yourself from other's influence.

To start this practice, relax your body as you usually do to enter the astral plane, through any of your preferred methods. Once your astral body starts to detach from your physical form, visualize yourself surrounded by peaceful and healing light. Set the intention of your journey. In this case, it is releasing emotional attachments that negatively influence you.

Scan your energy field once your body is floating in the astral realm. Focus on each part of your body until you feel that certain areas hold an emotional connection with others. For example, as you explore your energy field, you may find certain parts, like your chest or shoulders, feeling heavy and filled with sadness. These areas are usually where the attachment is held and where your body feels it the most. When you identify these parts, visualize the connection like cords that connect you to the negative experiences or people. Observe these cords, acknowledge their pain, and know that this is your opportunity to let it go.

To break these connections, visualize a sword imbued with powerful healing energy specifically designed to break these cords. Hold the sword firmly with both hands and focus on one cord at a time. Begin to cut through them, and as you cut each one, feel the energy breaking from you.

Take all the time you need to break each cord and breathe slowly. Once you cut them all, visualize healing energy flowing into the areas where the cords were connected, and take a moment to acknowledge the freedom and lightness you now feel.

Once you have finished, imagine a strong shield being created around you to shield you from negative experiences. This shield will protect you from unhealthy attachments and keep your emotions and energy balanced.

Restoring the Aura in the Astral Plane

The aura is the energetic field surrounding every person's body, and its health and vibrancy are essential for overall well-being. A weak and imbalanced aura can leave you feeling disconnected from your true self, drained, and vulnerable. However, negative energy can affect the aura, which can impact your happiness and cause emotional imbalance.

In the astral realm, you can restore the strength and brightness of your aura and protect it from negative influences that may drain it. To do so, begin detaching your astral form from your body as usual. Once you feel the separation, focus on your aura by visualizing a field of energy surrounding your body. The color and intensity of the light from your aura reflect your emotional and mental state. If your aura appears to be dim or the light is not strong enough, it means that there is an imbalance in the energy that needs to be restored. Begin your healing process by taking deep breaths. With every inhale, positive energy enters your aura and brightens its light bit by bit, and with every exhale, the negativity is released from your aura.

As you continue to restore your aura, imagine the colors becoming clearer and brighter. And when you heal all the dim spots, visualize a golden shield surrounding your aura. This shield will act as a protective barrier from any negative influence entering your field and keep your aura safe and bright.

Chapter 7: Connecting with Spirit Guides and Higher Beings

Connecting with spirit guides and higher beings in the astral plane can be incredibly beneficial for your learning experience. This chapter will introduce you to the concept of spirit guides as non-physical entities dedicated to assisting individuals in their life journey. Besides teaching you how to recognize their presence, the chapter will also offer several techniques for forming a connection with your spiritual guides.

Who Are the Spirit Guides?

Spirit guides are beings who can offer spiritual guidance and wisdom. Many have transcended to the highest level of spiritual growth and are now tasked with supporting people through their life journeys. Some are assigned to one person's soul, while others oversee many souls and communicate with beings on different levels and in different realms.

Several kinds of angels play different roles to guide you.[17]

You can have more than one spirit guide, as some are only temporary, only helping you through a challenging period. Others remain with you throughout your life and beyond, forever assigned to your soul's mission.

The rank of spirit guides includes a variety of higher beings, like helper, guardian archangels, ascended masters, elementals, spirit animals, and departed loved ones.

Archangels

As angelic leaders with massive energetic influence, archangels can bring powerful energy shifts into your life (including your travels to the astral realm). Each archangel oversees a special group of powers/requests from countless other lesser beings. For example, Archangel Michael's specialty is protection – he is often called on by individuals who wish to be shielded by Michael's energy during their spiritual explorations.

Guardian Angels

Unlike archangels, who look over many beings and people, guardian angels only have one charge. They devote their lives to guiding the soul and can be called upon at any time for help. While they may not be as powerful as archangels, their presence can be reassuring, especially because they are always ready to assist. You can call on them for any question or inquiry you may have about astral projection, and they will do their best to help you understand the process.

Helper Angels

These angels do not have assigned tasks but oversee many people and can offer help when no other angelic or other higher being is available. They are always on standby and will help with specific situations, even if it is only to get in touch with an archangel whose assistance you seek.

Ascended Masters

Former humans who have reached the highest level of spirituality, the ascended masters, have attained enlightenment and can help others work toward the same goal. Some of the most famous examples are Mother Mary and Buddha, spiritual leaders from two different religions and cultural backgrounds who lived their lives thriving for spiritual growth and influencing others. They have become leaders of the spiritual world and can be called upon for assistance in any aspect of spiritual exploration. They can be powerful allies during astral projection, especially if you are using your practice for spiritual growth.

Spirit Animals

Besides your pets who passed away, spirit animals can also be any other animals you feel drawn to. Either way, like angels, spirit animals are there to teach and guide people. You can have multiple spirit animals and meet them at any time, including while astral projecting.

Elementals and Interdimensional Beings

Elemental beings can assist if your inquiry is related to nature and its forces. Interdimensional beings, on the other hand, communicate with entities from different realms. They can facilitate the exploration of the astral planes, starting by helping you navigate the astral state.

Departed Loved Ones and Ancestors

Recently departed lovers can offer practical advice for exploring the land of the spirits. You may encounter them on the astral planes where they await you, ready to share their wisdom. Likewise, far-away ancestors (even some people you never knew who were related to you) can also be your spirit guides. You may be able to harness their collective wisdom to guide you on any path truly inspired to follow in the astral and physical realms.

Why Connect with Spirit Guides

After learning about all these types of spirit guides, you may wonder why you should or want to reach out to them. The purpose of connecting with spirit guides or higher beings is multifaceted.

Guidance

As their name implies, spiritual guides can be a massive source of guidance - and not just for spiritual growth. They can help you when you feel you are at a crossroads or facing a seemingly insurmountable obstacle. Have trouble finding your life purpose? Spirit guides can show you what resonates with you the most so you can align your actions to lead you to this purpose.

Healing

Many spiritual seekers are driven to this path because they need emotional or energetic healing. With their unique energetic signature, spirit guides can mend any energetic imbalance, helping you recover from traumas and experiences caused by negative energies. They can also provide guidance on how to cope with and move on from emotionally challenging situations.

Understanding of the Higher Truths

Spiritual guides have higher vibrational frequencies. By attuning to theirs, you will automatically connect to higher frequencies, which will help elevate yours. Besides energetic empowerment, spiritual guides can impart wisdom, shedding light on universal truths that can facilitate spiritual growth.

Communication

Lastly, your spiritual guides are your messengers in the spiritual/astral realm. They can communicate messages containing answers to your questions and problems - either to and from them or other spiritual guides. They may also provide insights on topics you have started exploring, even without you asking them. Spiritual guides assigned to you are attuned to your needs and interests and often know you need something before you do.

How to Recognize Spirit Guides as Astral Beings

While they may use unique ways to communicate with you in the astral realm, your spirit guides will send you unmistakable signs of their presence (sometimes even when you are not looking for them).

Here are some signs of the presence of spirit guides in the astral realm:

- **Vivid lights:** Since they know you rely on your imagination and visual senses, spirit guides in the astral realm will happily send you lights, colors, and other visual effects to make their presence known.

- **Sounds:** Ringing phones and music on the radio or television are the spirit guides' favorite ways to communicate. They can also do this in the astral realm, making these sounds appear in your visions.

- **Scents:** Spirits of deceased loved ones may try to communicate through olfactory messages, sending you odors you may be familiar with and associate with them. This is their way of letting you know who you are talking to.

- **Warm or cold feeling:** If you experience a sudden rise or drop in temperature while traveling, this may be your spirit guide communicating their presence. In most cases, they will send warmth to reassure you of their support and love.

- **A feeling of peace and love:** Likewise, feeling suddenly at peace when you were worked up or unsure just moments before can mean there is a spirit guide at work. They are telling you everything will be okay and you should continue your journey.

- **Symbolic visions of them:** Some spirit guides will send messages in the form of symbols and signs you notice in your vision. These can appear in front of your mind's eye randomly and several times until you get the message.

- **Sudden sensations:** If a spirit guide wants to get your attention to tell you something important, they might cause a sudden jolt or other surprising sensation. They do not do this to scare you but to make sure you notice them. They might cause you to stop while moving or propel you in a direction you have not intended to go.

- **Feeling you are not alone:** Sometimes, the only sign of an astral spirit being close to you is the feeling that you are not alone. This can be reassuring because you will know whoever is with you will follow you on your journey if you need assistance.
- **Sign from nature:** Some signs of spirit guides will be more subtle, especially if a spirit animal or elemental guide sends them. They may send you other animals, plants, and other symbolic elements of nature. For example, a spirit animal may try to get your attention by sending you visions of your current pets.

You can only rely on your spirit guide and learn from them if you know what they are trying to communicate with you. To receive, recognize, and reciprocate the messages you receive from your spirit guides in the astral realm, you must set clear intentions for doing so. Most will love to interact with you, but if you feel that you need protection while communicating with any being, feel free to ask while setting your intention of reaching out. It will make you feel safer and help you build relationships with your guides.

You must learn how to trust your gut to decode signs and symbols sent by spirit guides. The interaction between yourself and your guide is highly personal – and so is the process of deciphering the messages they send you. Spirit guides will send messages targeting what resonates with you, but you also must understand what they will be targeting.

Genuine guides will always approach you with the intent to help and never to cause confusion or fear. If you are unsure of what a guide is trying to tell you, try building a closer relationship with them. You can do this by asking them questions about them, the reason for meeting you on your journey, and asking for assistance every time you project. Doing so will establish a rapport where you can learn their communication pattern and what they are trying to communicate with the different signs and symbols.

Setting Intentions for Connection

Setting specific intentions is crucial for effective communication with spirit guides. By declaring your intention, you are clarifying what you are asking for and why. While they might be attuned to you, spirit guides will appreciate it when you ask for something specific because it shows them exactly how to help you. So, do not hesitate to ask by setting a clear intention.

In the astral world, you rely on your intuition, while your intention is the manifestation of your intuitive desires. By simply setting the intention to meet a spirit guide, you are making it known that you want to get in touch with them. They will come without you having to look for them. It works the same as any other intention. Keep it in mind, and your spirit guides will sense it.

Be open to hearing back from them and show this in your intention. If you have not met any spirit guide yet, be open to meeting anyone that comes your way. For example, you can say something like:

"I seek guidance for my highest good" or "I invite benevolent and loving energies into my experience."

Doing this before you begin your astral journey is best, but repeating these and similar affirmations while projecting does not hurt.

Calling on Astral Spirit Guides

Are you wondering how to call on astral spirit guides? Here is a guided meditation visualization that can help you meet and connect with your assigned spirit guide.

Instructions:
1. Make yourself comfortable, close your eyes, and take deep breaths. As you breathe out, let yourself sink deeper into the relaxation.
2. Focusing on your energy (whether sensing or seeing it around your astral body), let your imagination lead you to the astral realm.
3. Continue focusing on your energy as you travel to a tranquil, luminous area in the astral plane. Suddenly, you are standing in a glowing meadow, feeling a slight breeze on your skin. You see leaves swaying, moved by the wind, making you relax even more.
4. Now, think of something that usually enhances your creative imagination. For example, this can be a scent, a sight, or a feeling. Let go of any prejudice, old memory, or negativity that might be holding you back from meeting your guide.
5. Call on your spirit guide as you stand in this sacred, healing meadow. You can do this mentally or by calling out to them aloud.

6. Observe your presence for the signs of your spirit guide's presence. They may leave you symbols and send you warm, loving energy, visions, or light. For example, you may suddenly notice a glowing door. As your eyes adjust to the light, your spirit guide steps out.
7. If your guide appears or sends a clear signal, greet them by saying:

    "Come to me, my guide. I welcome you and thank you for your presence."
8. You can also ask them who they are and what they are there to help you with (you can do this even if they do not appear; just send a subtle sign of their presence).
9. Once they answer your questions, thank them again and let them go.
10. Revere in the loving, protective energy they left behind and the wholeness it infuses through your entire being.

Astral Light Communication Exercise

Once in the astral realm, you may want to send a signal to benevolent beings that you are open to connecting with them.

Instructions:
1. After separation, focus on your surroundings. Channel relaxing thoughts and feel your energy.
2. Breathe in and out as you notice the energy coursing through your astral body.
3. Now, focusing on the energy around your heart chakra, visualize a beam of light suddenly bursting out of your chest.
4. Let the light envelop the surrounding plane. Infuse the light with positivity and love. Remember, positivity attracts positivity, and you have now set a landmark to which benevolent beings are bound to become attracted.
5. As you continue sending out the light, you may notice a pulse of energy coming toward you. This might be a response from your spirit guide, signaling that they got your message.
6. Or, if you do not feel anything, you may see a sign or even a figure appearing in your mind's eye. This may be another response and a more direct one.

7. Whether your guide appears, sends signs, or communicates through energy, this technique will help you identify them and build trust in their presence.

Invoking Archangel Michael for Protection

Want to meet one of the most powerful protectors in the spiritual world? Call on Archangel Michael. Besides lending you his shield to repel unwanted energies, he can also provide you with a source of empowerment during projection.

Instructions:

1. Before entering the astral realm, set an intention to connect with Michael. Infuse your intention with a wish that comes from your heart.
2. If you are nervous about meeting him, light a candle or incense to help you relax before making contact.
3. Relax and enter the astral realm. Once you do, visualize a radiant blue light enveloping your body. This is Michael's calling card.
4. You may feel warm and protected. If you do, the archangel is now in your presence.
5. Tell him what you need protection from. You can say it out loud or create a vision that lets him know what dangers you may be facing.
6. If you do not know what you need protection from, you can ask for guidance or support along your journey.
7. Whatever you are asking for, focus your thoughts on this request.
8. Then, tell Michael what you will do next. Do you have an idea how you will protect yourself? If so, you can ask him to back up the protection with his power. Visualize the blue light seeping into your energy body, creating an impenetrable shield around you.
9. If you are unsure what actions you will take next, ask Michael to accompany you. He will observe you and your actions and guide you to take the appropriate steps. You can even ask him to make the first step to ensure you're going in the right direction. Ask for a sign, a word, or anything that will signal his response to you.
10. Then, express your gratitude for Michael's protection and assistance. You can do this by simply sending out thoughts and

feelings of gratitude through your energetic connection with him.

Group Guidance from Astral Beings

While you will rarely meet more than one spirit guide on your astral journey, this does not mean you cannot call on several of them at once. If you need lots of empowerment, you may benefit from procuring guidance from a group of benevolent astral beings.

Instructions:

1. Get comfortable, close your eyes, and breathe deeply to relax.
2. Formulate the intention of calling on spirit guides who can provide you with the assistance you need. Ideally, the more specific you are, the better. However, if you are unsure of what you need, simply make an intention to connect with beings who can offer love, guidance, and wisdom. For example, you can say:

   "I intend to call on all the loving and wise guides that can come to my aid."

   "I intend to receive assistance and guidance from all the angels and guides who are available to help."

3. For a more specific intention, you can say something like:

   "I intend to receive guidance for relaxation."

   "I intend to harness information about (insert topic), and I need all my guides to help me with this."

4. Take the journey to the astral realm.
5. Once there, visualize yourself standing in a circular room filled with lights and warmth.
6. Focus on your intention and send it toward the guides you want to call upon. Signal that you are open to their guidance. If your mind steers away from your intent (perhaps because you are nervous about meeting your guides), recenter your attention and refocus on communicating your intention once again.
7. At this point, your guides might appear, and you may be able to discern your guide's figures, or you may only see them represented as beams of light.
8. Ask them for what you need. Tell them to show you a sign that they have received your request.

9. Then, wait for their response. Be open to whatever you receive because their response may not be as specific as your questions were. They might communicate by sending you energy pulses, light flashes, or visions. If you feel warm and reassured, it means they have heard you, and you know their blessing and support.

10. Group guidance can be reassuring or give you more clarity on navigating the projection process. Once they answer your inquiries, ask your guides if they have any messages for you.

11. Then, wait again, allowing some time to pass to see whether they send you any sign or nudge that may signal a new message. They may not have anything else to tell you beyond what you asked, but they might have if they feel you need more guidance.

12. Lastly, once you ask for anything you wish and receive their response and any additional messages, thank your guides for coming to you.

13. Release them with thoughts/words of love and thank them for their assistance in advance. For example, you can say:

"I now release all my guides. Thank you for coming to meet me, listening to me, and offering your help in front of this council."

14. Watch them leave the circular room while continuing to revere in their warm light and energy.

Creating a Sacred Astral Meeting Space

Having a sacred space in the astral realm would give you the opportunity to have a safe melting point with your spiritual guide. It can also be a landmark for navigating astral planes. For example, you can envision this sacred place after your first separation, project there, and then make the next step from there.

Instructions:

1. Before separation, create an intention of setting up a sacred astral space. This can be an altar, a sanctuary, or a simple setting that makes you feel relaxed and centered. To form the intention, consider where you usually travel astrally (or where you would like to travel if you are new to projection). How do you prefer to interpret the messages you receive while traveling? For example, do you spend more time in the astral state to mull over the messages, or do you prefer to return and analyze them in the

physical world? What do you want to learn about? Do you seek spiritual growth? Answer these questions to form an intent aligned with your needs and preferences.

2. Ascend into the astral realm and visualize a relaxing setting. Take eight deep breaths and let your exhales center your mind. Then, you will get to designing.

3. Based on your intention, what do you imagine your sacred space should look like? For example, if you are used to interpreting messages in the astral world, you want it to be filled with everything that relaxes you. These can be signs, sounds, smells, warmth, etc.

4. Visualize a cozy space filled with radiant energy. When you look up, all you see is white light. When you look down, you see a white light at your feet. It feels peaceful and energetically protected.

5. For added reassurance, ask for a guide or two to reinforce your creation. Or, if you feel confident, call all the spirit guides. Introduce them to your sacred space and tell them you would like them to join you here in the future.

6. Ask your guides for the protection of your sacred space. Visualize a shield forming around it, fortified with your guides' protection.

7. Take in the sight of your sacred space. Next time you want to meet your guides or need a safe space in the astral realm, your sanctity will be there waiting for you. All you need to do is to think of it, and you will be projected there.

Chapter 8: Coming Home from Astral Travel

Grounding and centering yourself are crucial in your ability to process and learn from the insights you have gained during your journeys. You will receive tips on how to do this and balance your energy body to ensure that no harmful influences will affect you after your trip.

The Effects of Returning from the Astral Plane

You have prepared for your trip meticulously. You have used physical and mental relaxation and focusing techniques to ensure your transition to the astral state and journey in the astral realms will be fruitful. However, what about your return? Preparing and taking the necessary steps in the aftermath of your travel is crucial to maintain energetic balance and well-being.

You have to follow a certain routine after returning from the astral plane.[18]

Even if you prepare yourself before your journey with meditation or any other deep relaxation method, you may feel disoriented and drained afterward. This is normal, and everyone practicing astral projection experiences this from time to time. The process profoundly affects your psyche, which is why you feel slightly (or more than slightly) off.

You may feel detached from your body even after reuniting with it because your astral self was so deeply affected that it cannot fully break away from the otherworldly experience. You may also feel exhausted physically and spiritually. While your physical body was not participating in the travel itself, it remained connected to your energy – and because your energy body was affected, so was your physical body.

It is a good idea to initiate a projection attempt when you are well rested but it's equally important to de-stress after, too. Your body, mind, and spirit need time to adjust and recover. If you do not take time to rest (even if you do not attempt another trip anytime soon), you will continue to feel drained and off. This can hinder your learning experience and any future attempts at astral projection.

Many experience symptoms across the body, mind, and spirit, collectively known as *astral fatigue*. Most practitioners describe it as an overwhelming feeling of lack of energy and disorientation. How affected you are may depend on your experience, how you prepare yourself, whether you take time off to rest, and how many projection attempts you make within a short period.

Seasoned travelers can channel their willpower to avoid astral fatigue and focus on remembering the insights they have gained during their journey. How? The astral body is still closely tethered to the physical body for beginners. You need this connection to have an anchor point and remain centered for safe travel and return. With practice, you can separate your astral body from the physical body further away, so your physical body will not be affected as much during your travels.

Similarly, experienced travelers can make several attempts quickly without experiencing astral fatigue, while beginners cannot. As a novice, you are likely to be very used to being in your physical body, so navigating movement in your astral state will come at a higher cost. Your trips will be shorter, and you will feel more drained afterward. This is all normal, but it gets easier with time.

Fortunately, there is a lot you can do to diminish the effects of astral fatigue and boost your recovery and learning experience. For example, setting an intention (yes, the intention is a magic word here, too) to clear your mind just before you return can be helpful to make the re-entry easier for your body and mind. This will allow you to focus on becoming fully present in the physical body while still retaining what you have learned without letting your astral experience affect your physical body.

Meditation may help you relax if you feel disoriented and confused after your return. You do not have to do it immediately when rejoining your body. Do a quick grounding exercise right after, then a slightly longer meditation a few hours later. Take it slow the next day to recover from any physical and mental symptoms you may have experienced.

Do something nice for yourself. When you feel out of balance after a powerful energetic experience, acts of self-care will work wonders for speeding up your recovery. Go for a walk, cook, play with your pet, take a relaxing bath, or do whatever you feel like doing. The goal is to relax and make yourself feel loved and cherished.

Listen to your body and mind. If you listen to their signals carefully, they will tell you what they need (and do not need). They will let you know when you are ready to continue your practice and when you need more time off.

Nourish your body and soul with nutritious food, proper hydration, and light exercise. While rest is fundamental, physical activity is just as vital for your health and well-being. You can have both with low-impact exercises that will not drain you additionally.

Besides the effects on your body, mind, and spirit, astral projection will profoundly impact your emotional landscape. You might experience many positive and negative emotions during your travels. Both can be distracting and overpowering, so you must process them to avoid disbalance or becoming overwhelmed. For example, as thrilling as it is to finally experience the interconnectedness with the other realms, the feeling that you are linked to everything and everyone can hit you quite hard.

One of the best ways to deal with the emotions you will encounter is to reflect on them. Journaling is a wonderful tool for emotional reflection, especially if writing about your feelings is easier than talking about them. You just have to let your intuition guide you and write about your feelings while traveling. Make sure to mention both positive and negative feelings. Reflect on why you may have had them and what this could mean for you.

Other quiet reflection tools may also work for recording and understanding the lessons you have learned and the emotions you have experienced. For example, you can use the 3-2-1 method. It is simple.

Instructions:
1. Write down three takeaways from your experience. Then, based on those, ask yourself two questions. For example, you can ask yourself what you have learned or how best to handle your emotions.
2. Finally, determine one action step for moving forward. For instance, you can plan to integrate the knowledge you have gained into your life or prepare yourself to handle your emotions slightly better next time.

Grounding Techniques

Grounding is just as essential after coming from astral travel as it is before leaving for it. The goal is to make you feel focused, which will help you process, analyze, and integrate what you have learned in the astral plane into the physical realm.

Numerous grounding and re-centering techniques can help you balance your energy body after an astral journey. One of the easiest ones is simply reconnecting with the natural world by walking or standing barefoot. You will simply need to find a patch of nature, take off your shoes, and stand or walk in it, reveling in the connection between your body and nature.

Grounding and Re-Centering Exercise

This exercise will help you ground and re-center yourself in just a few minutes after returning to the physical plane. It is great if you feel unsettled or disoriented after reuniting with your body.

Instructions:

1. As soon as you become fully aware of your physical body, take a deep breath through your nostrils and close your eyes. Sitting or standing with your feet touching the ground is best.
2. After inhaling, pause and hold your breath for 4 seconds to open up your chest as much as possible. Then, release your breath slowly and gently.
3. Continue breathing with the same patterns for a few more breaths.
4. Raise your arms above your head, palms upwards, as if pushing toward the sky. You can even stand on your toes to give yourself a little leverage to "push."
5. Let your arms fall to your side and relax your entire body.
6. Repeat steps 4 and 5 two more times. Feel the tension easing from your body before continuing.
7. Imagine roots sprouting from your feet and into the ground, connecting you to the depth of the earth and nature's energy.
8. Palms facing down, raise your arms in front of your belly, and start moving them in a clockwise direction in front of you. As you do this, visualize drawing energy from the earth's core to restore your energetic balance.
9. As you do the circles, start shifting your balance from one leg to another as if tracing the path of the energy you are harnessing through your feet. You can feel the energy rising under and around you as if standing in water.
10. Continue channeling the energy upward with the concentric motions of your hands.
11. If your mind begins to wander or becomes unsettled again, channel your focus back to your hands' movements in front of your belly.

12. Slow down and change directions after a few circles in a clockwise direction. Breathe deeply and enjoy your breathing and movement's relaxing and centering effect.
13. Continue focusing on the present moment and the feeling of energy traveling upwards from your feet to your center.
14. After a few circles in the opposite direction, stop your hands directly in front of your belly.
15. Move them toward you and slightly upward, as if moving the energy from around you to you.
16. Breathe in and breathe out as you repeat the previous step 5-10 times.
17. Let your breathing return to normal, and place your hands on the center of your body. Enjoy the feeling of groundedness and being present in your physical body.

Setting Healthy Boundaries for Astral Travel

While practice makes perfect, this does not mean you have to overexert yourself while trying to master astral projection. There is no need to take frequent trips because they will not allow you to learn more anyway. Instead, set boundaries for a regular but healthy astral travel schedule.

Give yourself enough time to process, analyze, and learn from the information you have learned on your journeys. Besides your mind, your body and energy will also need time to recover between travels. When you feel drained, you cannot expect to focus and pick up any new information. You will just get frustrated and lose confidence in your ability to astral project and grow spiritually.

If you had a particularly eventful journey (even if it was mainly positive), you may want to take more time after it. After all, you will have more information to process and more energetic influences to deal with. On the other hand, if you did not have many interactions or experiences on your journey, your recovery time will be shorter, too.

If you have established communication with your spirit guide, you should not let too much time pass between your interactions. It is also understandable if you are eager to learn more about your guide or uncover the secrets of the astral realm itself. The key here is to find the balance between what serves you and what causes you to feel drained.

Aura Cleansing

Energies you interact with can infuse your aura, training your energy and leaving you out of balance. Over time, they can drain you of your energy and even seep into your environment. As your energy drains, you will not have enough of it coursing through your aura (energy body).

If you do not expel negativity regularly, your aura may start to look more like a dim light bulb rather than the radiant light sphere it can be. Dimming in your aura will come in parallel with the low vibrational levels, preventing you from focusing your mind during astral travel and everyday life. Worse, nothing will attract negative entities more in your travels than carrying tons of negative baggage yourself.

Here is a great way to prevent all of this. You will need a bowl, salt, and water. Optionally, you can prepare a smudge stick, incense, and crystals for energy cleansing.

Instructions:

1. Fill the bowl with salt and water and place it on the table before you. It will absorb the negative energies about to leave your energy body.
2. Light an incense or smudge stick for relaxation and to help you connect to your consciousness. These are great for cleaning space, too, so they will eliminate energetic distractions and prompt you to focus on cleaning your aura.
3. Sit comfortably and take a few deep breaths.
4. Join the fingers of your left hand and bring them to the side of your face (just above your forehead). Repeat the same with the fingers on your other hand.
5. After holding the fingers on both sides of your head for 15 seconds, let your arms fall to the side and visualize a sphere of soft light glowing around your body. Imagine this light slowly expanding and clearing any stagnant or negative energy in your aura.
6. As the light travels through your body, you may notice that some areas feel heavier; this is because the energy in these areas is unbalanced.
7. Bring your fingers to your head again (like in step 3) and visualize your aura expanding and filling the heavy spots with love, earth,

and light energy.

8. As vitality is restored to these spots, your energy body starts to glow even brighter. The energy flow across your aura has now been rebalanced, and any negativity has been expelled.

9. Repeat this exercise after each projection attempt, even the ones you feel were unsuccessful. You never know what you picked up while navigating separation and crossing to the astral realm. Change the bowl of salt water after every couple of uses. You do not want to keep all the negativity around you for too long.

Some other ways to cleanse your aura and energy body and set up boundaries for spiritual practices include the following.

Put Up a Mirror

Set your intention for your aura to act as a mirror against negativity. This way, it will repel unwanted energies and influences in any realm. You can still choose to allow in beneficial energies and every influence aligned with your highest good. Moreover, with a mirror-like aura, you can also reflect love, compassion, and positivity to those sending these to you while communicating. For example, when a spirit guide sends you these gifts, you can send them back, establishing a relationship based on mutual respect and understanding.

Listen to Your Reactions

Listen to your emotional and physical responses when cleansing your aura with a protective shield. How does detecting or repelling negativity in your auric field make you feel? Does any of it cause sensations in your body? Learning about your reactions to the influences will reinforce the connection between your physical, emotional, and spiritual self, making integrating what you learn in the astral state into your life and growth much easier. You will understand what energies serve and do not serve you if you know the responses they evoke in your body, mind, and heart.

Reinforce Your Intentions

As you have probably realized, intention plays a crucial role in every step of the astral projection process. Setting the right intention can make a huge difference from preparation to analyzing what you have learned on your journey. So, reinforce your intention for spiritual growth and repel anything that may prevent this every time you return from an astral voyage. For example, you can say:

"I intend to take away from this experience only what serves me and leave behind everything that doesn't."

Use Your Hands

Did you know that the easiest way to interact with your energy is through your hands? If you feel overwhelmed after reuniting with your body and cannot focus on visualizing your entire aura, use your hands instead. Focus on feeling your energy emanating from them and moving them around your body, as if painting the outline of your energy body. This will make it easier to visualize it because you will feel the energy around you and have something to focus on.

Cleanse Your Space Too

Energies you pick up might jump quickly into your space, so cleanse your surroundings, too, and not just your aura. Otherwise, the energies can reattach themselves to your aura, and your cleansing will be in vain. You can purify your space with crystals like obsidian, which repels negativity – or try rose quartz, which invites love and positivity. You could choose to use a smudge stick or spray to chase away the negative influences attached to you and your space.

Check Your Aura Regularly

Even if you do not feel that you picked up any negative influences in either realm (yes, you can carry them from the physical world to the astral realms and vice versa), you should still regularly do a quick aura sweep. You will want to check the unwanted energies before they take hold and start causing imbalances and other hindrances in your well-being.

Integrating Insights Through Journaling

Record your experience right after returning from your astral journey. This is when your memory of them is freshest in your mind. While you are unlikely to forget the experience, some details may fade with time, especially if your journey was eventful.

Keep a dedicated journey for astral projection, and write down any messages, symbols, emotions, and thoughts you had during each voyage. Did any of them stand out for some reason? If so, do you know why? Were you able to decipher the signs you have received?

Even if you cannot interpret something right away, you should still write it down. You can always reread and analyze your entries later, perhaps after gaining deeper insight into the issue. Returning to earlier records will allow you to summarize the insights and wisdom you have harnessed.

Reflect on what happened on each projection attempt, whether you have received any messages or signs or had profound emotional experiences. For example, ask yourself: "What did I learn during this journey?" or "How can I integrate these insights into my everyday life?" The ultimate goal of astral projection is to encourage growth and spiritual liberation. What you learn on your travels can go a long way to achieving this if you record them.

Did you know that recording your astral lessons has another benefit, too? It gets you into the habit of actively learning from your experiences. Each time you write about feelings, messages, or signs you have, you will need to evoke them so their details become clear in your mind. This will help you remember exactly how you experienced them while traveling and analyze their meaning.

Once you have them in your mind and have analyzed them, you can write them down in your journal. The more you do this, the easier it will become to gain clarity on what you have learned and remember the details of your experience.

With regular astral journaling, you will see patterns emerge. You can then analyze these patterns and see whether they also have meaning in the physical realm. It opens up a deeper understanding of the interconnectedness of body and spirit and the realms the latter can cross and linger in.

Protective Visualization

Just as you would need to protect your energy before your journey, so would doing a protective visualization upon your return benefit you. During your travels, you will interact with different energies and entities, engaging in an energy exchange (the same way it happens when you engage with people and your environment in the physical world). These interactions can profoundly affect you energetically, emotionally, and physically.

Moreover, by returning with negative influences attached to you, your energy and well-being will be continually affected in the physical realm. It can continue draining your energy and even affect others around you. After all, these influences feed on energy and will seek out and take advantage of any source they can get to.

By casting a protective bubble around after reuniting with your physical self, you can repel and keep away those harmful, energetic influences you picked up along the way. It will stop the negative energies from infusing and affecting yours and bringing your vibrational frequency down.

Instructions:

1. Get comfortable, close your eyes, and sit in the calm for one to two minutes.
2. Imagine a bright protective light emerging from your belly and enveloping you. It can be any color (white, blue, violet, golden, etc.) – choose the one that resonates with you. Why not test the different colors and see what works best for you? When you find the one that feels the most comforting, stick with it.
3. See this bright light expand around your physical body, reaching a light distance from it as if infusing all layers of the aura body.
4. You may find that the shield looks a little weaker in some places. This can happen if your experiences were particularly draining, you had interactions with a negative energy/entity, or you did not protect yourself sufficiently before your journey. The negativity took hold of your energy body, taking out chunks of your protective shields.
5. Visualize sending bursts of white light toward these parts. Infuse them with love and positive thoughts. It will repel the negativity and help you fill the gaps.
6. Continue until the protective bubble around you feels strong and impenetrable.
7. As you observe the light bubble surrounding you, imagine feeling enveloped in a big, warm blanket. It keeps you cocooned in and centered and your energy safe from external negative influences.
8. Repeat this exercise regularly to build an empowered energy body. If necessary, do it after every projection attempt, or even between them, when you analyze what you have learned on your travels.

Chapter 9: Cultivating a Lifelong Journey of Exploration

In this chapter, you will understand the importance of viewing astral projection and spiritual exploration as a life-long journey rather than a goal or destination. You will learn how to approach these practices as ongoing endeavors and understand why astral projection can completely transform your life. This chapter also delves into the relationship between meditation and astral projection and how to determine whether you are in the right mental headspace for transporting into an alternate state of consciousness. You will learn to establish consistent practices for astral travel and understand how practical exercises like gratitude and the Healing Temple can prepare you for astral practices.

The Life-Long Journey of Astral Projection

Astral projection is a life-long journey and an incredible life-altering tool. It can be used to learn invaluable lessons and constantly work toward being a better version of yourself. Unlike mastering a skill, there isn't a ceiling to what you can achieve with astral projection. You will never reach a moment when you no longer benefit from it.

Journeying through the astral realm will always add to your life. The things you see and experience are usually influenced by real events, thoughts, feelings, worries, and relationships. This means that astral projection can continuously help you make better decisions and see things from different perspectives, regardless of how well you have grasped the ability to journey into and out of the astral realm.

Astral projection requires a certain relaxed yet focused state of mind, which you can achieve through meditation. Meditating regularly allows you to stay mindful, grounded, and calm and trains you to continuously reflect on your thoughts, emotions, and experiences. Maintaining this headspace and approach to life enhances your interactions with yourself, others, and the world around you. This is why you should always consider astral projection a journey rather than a destination.

Focus on the Process, Not the Outcome

Being able to easily transport between the realms is an important skill, especially if you wish to incorporate astral projection into your routine. However, focusing on being able to do it as quickly as you can may hinder your progress. Pressuring yourself prevents you from getting into a meditative state. It also subconsciously makes you less receptive to the knowledge you will gain through the practice after mastering it. You will inadvertently lose interest because, in your mind, you have already reached your goal and will feel compelled to seek out another challenge.

On the other hand, viewing astral projection as a life-long journey allows you to maintain your excitement toward it. You will realize that even if you are seamlessly traveling between the realms and can drift into the astral realm on cue, there is still so much to learn. You will understand that all sessions are equally beneficial and unique. When exploring the world of astral projection, you should always focus on learning.

Understand That All Attempts Are Valuable

View all your attempts and experiences as opportunities to understand the world, yourself, and your consciousness more deeply. Appreciate and enjoy the entire process, from when you close your eyes and practice meditation to when you return to your body. All occurrences and obstacles you face during your journey, whether struggling to meditate, unable to achieve vivid visualizations, or feeling lost in the astral realm, are valuable. They will encourage you to think of ways to improve next time and bring your attention to internal or external factors that might be holding you back.

The entire process of astral projection, whether you reach the "destination" or struggle to find your way into the astral realm, is a stepping stone toward achieving personal and spiritual growth. Prioritize development overreaching your goals. Celebrate even the smallest instances of growth, such as unlocking a deeper relaxation or meditative state or having clearer visualizations. While these might seem like small milestones in the journey of astral projection, they count the most. You cannot voyage into the astral realm without unlocking a deep meditative state or gaining clarity in your visualizations. Acknowledging that every step counts allows you to focus on preparing and practicing instead of emphasizing the outcome.

Your Goals Aren't Everything

As counter-intuitive as it sounds, drawing your attention away from the end goal leads to better outcomes. Purposefully integrate the skills you learn while preparing for astral projection and the insights you obtain during the practice. Astral projection is an intriguing undertaking that everyone would feel curious to experience at least once in their lifetime. However, if you are picking up this practice as part of your spiritual growth journey, doing it passively will not help.

Make the Most of Your Insights

Use the insights you gain to enhance your awareness, emotional balance, and daily life. View this as an opportunity to build healthier relationships and improve mindfulness and intuition. Most importantly, strive to achieve a balance between astral projection and the real world.

View It as a Complement, Not an Escape

Some people fall into the trap of turning to the astral realm to escape from the physical. Approach this practice with mental and emotional clarity and use it to complement your physical life rather than replace it.

Be Curious and Embrace the Experience

Keep an open mind and heart when delving into astral projection. You might learn more and be exposed to more dimensions of experience than you expect. Instead of closing yourself off to your initial expectations or what you think you only need to learn, embrace the evolution of the journey and the influx of knowledge, exposure, and wisdom you'll gain. Go into each session feeling curious and perceiving it as a new opportunity for self-discovery.

Don't Look for Specific Results

Don't limit yourself by seeking out specific results, and let go of any expectations you might have. Accept that the astral realm will offer what you need instead of what you seek, so do not be disappointed if you do not find what you are searching for. To reap the benefits of astral projection, you must view it as a journey that will help you evolve, grow, and deepen your understanding throughout your life. It is an unending endeavor of self-discovery that will help bring clarity throughout all stages of your life.

Why Astral Projection Is a Transformative Process

It Can Shift Your Energy

Astral projection can significantly enrich your life and bring meaning to it due to the profound, deeper, and all-embracing understanding of your life and the entirety of existence. It allows you to get attuned to your energy on all levels and manage your energetic state throughout the day.

Your energy can impact your thoughts, feelings, and mood. It also affects your productivity, decision-making abilities, and interactions. Being connected to your energy will allow you to enhance all aspects of your life. The astral realm exposes you to the fears and shadows that hinder your growth and hold you back from unlocking your potential. Facing these fears is integral to your healing and development journey.

It Changes Your Perception of Death

Astral projection also offers a sense of peace and relief. The ability to transition into other-worldly realms proves the belief that consciousness extends beyond the physical. While astral projection does not mimic what is to come after death, it can help demystify and prepare you for this transition.

It Naturally Aligns with Your Beliefs

Astral projection is not one-size-fits-all. Each person's journey and experience with this practice is unique, depending on their life's circumstances. Therefore, it can be aligned with your beliefs. You can complement your spiritual beliefs and knowledge with the insights and revelations you make during your astral travels to grasp an understanding of the universe that makes sense to you.

It Encourages You to Tap into Your Intuition

No matter how many scientific breakthroughs and groundbreaking discoveries are made, the collective rational mind will not apprehend all the secrets and inner workings of existence. Therefore, you cannot rely solely on your rational mind and your worldly consciousness. Practicing astral projection teaches you to merge your ability to think rationally and the capacity to tap into your intuition to make the best decisions. It allows you to balance your physical and non-physical consciousness and analytical and emotional tendencies in all aspects of your life.

It Expands Your Consciousness

Astral projection can significantly expand your consciousness. When your brain actively engages with an other-worldly environment, you will inadvertently tap into your intuition and creativity. Exploring an aspect of existence you know nothing about forces you to rely on skills other than knowledge. Normally, creative thinking, gut feelings, and visionary thinking complement wisdom and background information. However, when dealing with the unknown, all your senses are heightened to help you make the best judgment and navigate accordingly.

Meditation, Astral Projection, and Universal Exploration

When your astral projection voyage sets sail, you will inadvertently find yourself experimenting with different environments and techniques to help you achieve the most conducive state for astral travel. You could try to turn down the lights, try different essential oils, change your position, or explore various meditation techniques.

It's not unnatural for astral projection enthusiasts to grow familiar with meditative techniques used in varying belief systems, from Hinduism to Sufism. Not only does this allow them to master the art of meditation, but it also expands their knowledge of and experience with different belief systems. This expansion of wisdom can deepen their understanding of the universe or offer perspective on certain things.

Through this effort of meditative exploration, some people discover that even belief systems that might seem so dissimilar at a surface level are usually rooted in similar ideas or teachings or simply have a comparable essence. This makes people more understanding and tolerant of those with different backgrounds and convictions and helps them grasp the concept of collective consciousness.

This concept is the idea that all beings are interconnected through universal awareness. Understanding this concept helps you achieve emotional balance, enhances empathy, and allows you to understand that you are a part of the larger whole. It also teaches you the importance of living harmoniously with nature and other beings around you, cultivating your sense of purpose. The concept of universal awareness also supports your astral projection efforts because it helps you realize that you are interacting with a collective, unified field of consciousness while exploring this astral realm. This helps you feel more at ease when you are exploring the unknown and offers a greater sense of clarity.

How to Tell if You Are in the Right Mental Headspace

Practicing mindfulness and meditation techniques regularly allows you to connect with yourself, your consciousness, and the universe. You can tell you have cultivated this connection when you feel enlightened. Some astral projection practitioners describe it as a "lightbulb moment" where the profound realization of interconnectedness washes over them. You will gain a moment of clarity, knowing that "everyone is everyone, and everything is everything."

What you offer to others is an extension of offering the same for yourself. For instance, if you treat everyone with love, kindness, and respect, you will be pouring into your own cup. Ultimately, you must tear down the mental barrier that differentiates yourself and others. If you speak hatred to the world, it will reflect back to you. Inflicting pain on others would hurt you as well. Whatever you put out into the universe comes back to you. Your journey into the astral world is as about understanding the universe as it is about exploring yourself. It will open your mind to the fact that all beings are no more but a contribution to the collective consciousness.

Morality and Interconnectedness

Humans search for knowledge and yearn to build a deeper relationship with the universe. Since the beginning of time, the human spirit has been concerned with making sense of the world around it. Ancient peoples from all corners of the world made up stories about how and why the world was created to understand how everything came to be and what they were meant to do.

They even created rules that dictated what is acceptable and what is not to determine how they should interact with others and the world around them. If they made up the pantheons to which they prayed and made up laws that outlined what was acceptable and what was not, how did they collectively agree on what was right and what was wrong? Why did they decide that stealing is wrong and that being kind is right if they had no reference to turn to? It's because they understood the concept of interconnectedness. They knew that what they did and spoke out into the universe would return to them.

Maybe the reason why immorality is growing more and more common by the day is due to the soul-crushing nature of the capitalist world humans live in today. This fast-paced world has made stress and anxiety a normal state to live in. Most people operate in survival mode, having no time to process their thoughts, feelings, and circumstances. They no longer engage in things that fulfill their soul, nor do they explore, let alone ask questions about the universe. This is where astral projection comes in. It can offer a short yet deeply effective break from the demands of daily life. It provides a space where one can heal, understand, and connect. The effects of astral projection are not only experiences in the other-worldly realm, but its impact ripples into every aspect of one's existence.

Incorporating Consistent Astral Practices into Your Routine

Build Habits

Dedicate a specific time of your day for astral practices. Engaging in these practices in the morning will allow you to start your day on a positive note, setting the tone for what comes next. Alternatively, you can practice them before bed to help you unwind, clear your mind, and easily drift off to sleep.

- Meditation: Meditation can boost your focus and help you relax, preparing your mind, soul, and body for astral projection.
- Journaling: Journaling about your thoughts, feelings, and day allows you to identify patterns and growth areas in your life. This will allow you to make sense of your experiences in the astral realm and identify what you can learn from them.
- Setting intentions: Practice setting intentions throughout the day. Determine the purpose behind your actions and decisions. This will train your brain to navigate the astral realm purposefully and safely.

- Astral travel sessions: Schedule a specific time to engage in or attempt astral projection at least once a week. This will help you build familiarity with the experience and develop the ability to travel between alternate states of consciousness. Make sure to attempt astral travel at the time of day when you are typically relaxed to increase your chances of success.

Integrate Your Insights into Daily Life

Intentionally integrate your insights and what you have learned into your daily life. For instance, if you cultivate empathy, incorporate this trait into your relationships. If you have revelations regarding your career, consider using this guidance to achieve your goals and work toward unlocking your life's purpose.

Set a Sustainable Schedule

Make astral practices a regular part of your routine, but do not do them excessively. To maintain a sense of balance, engage in self-care practices such as grounding activities, getting plenty of rest, and eating a healthy diet.

Practice Gratitude

Practicing gratitude can help shift your attention from negative feelings and occurrences in your life. It compels you to think about the good things and trains you to notice the positive things you tend to overlook. You begin to see the silver lining in all situations, which eases your worries and allows you to get into a more relaxed state conducive to shifting to alternate states of consciousness. Approaching life with a more positive and grateful outlook can boost your mood and improve your overall health.

Here are some things you can do that will allow you to cultivate gratitude:

- Practice mindfulness: Slow down, engage your senses, and savor even life's smallest moments. This can help you appreciate the little things and pull you away from worrying and dwelling on negative thoughts. Mindfully direct your energy and focus on the positive things.
- Maintain a gratitude journal: At the end of each day, write about something or a moment that you appreciated. It does not have to be something major. It could simply be that you enjoyed the

weather or a baby smiling at you.

- Express your appreciation: Write notes of appreciation to your loved ones or verbally express these positive emotions.
- Actively reframe negative events: Reframe negative events or things you regret to determine the positive things about these experiences. You have learned something from it or ended up taking positive initiative as a result.

Enhance Your Astral Skills

Work on developing skills that can help you engage in astral projection more effectively. You can work with astral guides and learn to communicate with them, explore lucid navigation, do healing or energy work, or explore your past lives. You can also incorporate meditative visualization into your routine or use guided meditations. Make sure to evaluate your progress over time.

The Healing Temple Exercise

This exercise can help you create mental, emotional, and spiritual states needed to heal and restore your energy. Simply lie down in a comfortable and quiet position and breathe deeply. Clear your mind of any thoughts and bring your attention to your physical sensations and the present moment. Get into a meditative state, and then visualize your ultimate place of peace, joy, and comfort. It could be a welcoming, warm temple, endless lush forest, or serene beach. Once you are satisfied with your space, visualize healing energies or guides filling up the place. These guides and energies are there to help heal you mentally, emotionally, physically, and spiritually. Whenever you are ready, slowly bring your attention back to the present moment. Integrate this exercise into your routine, making sure to do it at least once a week to restore your energy and release negative feelings like stress and anxiety.

As you approach the end of this journey, you are ready to put all the knowledge and insights you have gained into practice. Embrace the revelations and transitions you will experience throughout your ongoing spiritual growth journey with an open mind and heart.

Conclusion

Many people are curious to try astral projection at least once in their lifetime. While it is an extremely enlightening experience, very few people realize that this practice should be approached as a lifelong journey rather than a destination so you can reap its transformative benefits. The astral realm is unique to everyone who experiences it. Your experience there is shaped by your circumstances, intentions, degree of openness, thoughts, feelings, worries, and relationships. This allows you to gain clarity and perspective to make the best decisions. Since what you see and encounter in your astral travels are ever-evolving according to where you are at that moment in life, this practice can help you work continuously toward becoming the best version of yourself.

Over time, your perception of existence, understanding of personal and collective consciousness, and experience with interconnectedness with the universe will all evolve. Each chapter in this book has served as a stepping stone in building your understanding of astral projection. It's time to put all this theoretical and practical knowledge into practice. Keep in mind that your first few astral projection attempts may be unsuccessful. However, maintaining a positive mindset, staying persistent, and following the instructions and tips in this book will allow you to safely and effectively drift into the astral state of consciousness.

This book has been your guide through exploring the astral realm. It aims to demystify the concept of astral projection by delving into the foundations, core principles, and historical roots of this endeavor. In the previous chapters, you have also learned how to prepare your mind, body, and environment for astral travel.

Maintaining the focused yet relaxed state of mind required for achieving out-of-body experiences is tricky. What works for others might not necessarily work for you, and you are likely to go through a lot of trial and error. You may have to experiment with different meditation techniques or change various things about your environment until you determine what is most conducive to this practice. You will know your meditation is effective when you get a lightbulb moment. You might suddenly experience the realization that everyone and everything in the world is interconnected.

The astral realm offers boundless opportunities for personal growth and development, healing, and spiritual connection. Mastering the art of drifting into and out of different states of consciousness gives you the power to transform your life. You will confidently gain perspective and clarity on different challenges, heal your emotional wounds, seek answers, unlock the universe's secrets, and build deep connections with your guides.

If you enjoyed this book, I'd greatly appreciate a review on Amazon because it helps me to create more books that people want. It would mean a lot to hear from you.

To leave a review:
1. Open your camera app.
2. Point your mobile device at the QR code.
3. The review page will appear in your web browser.

Thanks for your support!

Here's another book by Mari Silva that you might like

Your Free Gift
(only available for a limited time)

Thanks for getting this book! If you want to learn more about various spirituality topics, then join Mari Silva's community and get a free guided meditation MP3 for awakening your third eye. This guided meditation mp3 is designed to open and strengthen ones third eye so you can experience a higher state of consciousness. Simply visit the link below the image to get started.

https://spiritualityspot.com/meditation

Or, Scan the QR code!

References

5 Techniques to Experience Astral Projection. (2024). Anima Mundi Herbals. https://animamundiherbals.com/blogs/blog/5-techniques-to-experience-astral-projection?srsltid=AfmBOoqKtek1Y7DOmtuEpM2nnO-YgBsAbwKf1t9P575GlcbKKPrfg55G

A, M. (2023, December 18). *Encounters with Entities Astral Projection - Esoteric Befief.* Esoteric Befief. https://esotericbelief.com/encounters-with-entities-astral-projection

Aaron Abke. (2019, May 8). *How To Handle Negative Entities // Astral Projection 003.* YouTube. https://www.youtube.com/watch?v=DP4RJlYSbXI

admin-muskokayogafestival. (2024, April 16). *Astral Body (Emotional Energy Body) - Definition & Detailed Explanation - Chakras & Energy Glossary - muskokayogafestival.com.* Muskokayogafestival.com. https://muskokayogafestival.com/chakras-energy-glossary/astral-body-emotional-energy-body/

Agarwal, A. (2024). *The Astral Plane And Its Divisions.* Streetdirectory.com. https://www.streetdirectory.com/etoday/-eufuuo.html

Amar Singh Kaleka. (2017, November 16). *Hypnagogic Meditation (Lucid Dreaming) - Amar Singh Kaleka - Medium.* Medium. https://medium.com/@ArmKaleka/hypnagogic-meditation-lucid-dreaming-f6a71fdef98d

Ann-Murray Brown. (2024, December). *3-2-1 Reflection: A Facilitation Tool For Learning.* Linkedin.com. https://www.linkedin.com/pulse/3-2-1-reflection-facilitation-tool-learning-ann-murray-brown--2r1le/

Astral Projection Affirmations. (2024). Trinityaffirmations.com. https://www.trinityaffirmations.com/product/astral-projection-affirmations?srsltid=AfmBOoqSwo_6fj9adOlnbR1ir7g-RsiwCNUtaL9ZhPE9yZ9vvBUOptqO

Astral Projection Positive Affirmations - Free Affirmations - Free Positive Affirmations. (2024). Freeaffirmations.org. https://freeaffirmations.org/astral-projection-positive-affirmations

Astral Projection Vs Lvs. Lucid Dreaming Vs. Rvs. Reality Shifting. (2024). Shapedream.co. https://www.shapedream.co/lucid-dreaming/astral-projection-vs-lucid-dreaming-vs-reality-shifting

Astral Projection: The Ultimate Guide for Beginners. (2023). Tiny Rituals. https://tinyrituals.co/blogs/tiny-rituals/astral-projection?srsltid=AfmBOoqbePrMNkkitgzDa527fnrGE9PbWyYeyBJ_Ox2WkGQdFKxsNbsD

Astral, A. (2022, February 24). *Magick Makers.* Magick Makers. https://themagickmakers.com/blog/dreamwork-an-astral-projection-ritual?srsltid=AfmBOoqW7D9_MtHJB_Op_tiizu8XvFr5fhxxwOr0PkHNZJR7cFzxCWm_

AstralHQ Team. (2021, October 9). *How To Find Your SPIRIT GUIDES While Astral Projecting.* AstralHQ. https://astralhq.com/find-spirit-guides/

Bansal, N. (2024, December 5). *How Astral Projection Gave Me The Peace I Needed.* Education. https://vocal.media/education/how-astral-projection-gave-me-the-peace-i-needed

Benston, J. (2021, November 15). *Your energy is contagious and your reputation is at stake - Jane Benston.* Jane Benston. https://janebenston.com/your-energy-is-contagious-and-your-reputation-is-at-stake/

Brown, J. (2024, September 6). *20 Best Crystals for Astral Projection: Your Spiritual Guide.* Manifest Everyday. https://manifesteveryday.com/crystals-for-astral-projection/

Caro, T. (2020, December 6). *Your Spirit Guide is Trying to Contact You [Watch Signs].* Magickal Spot. https://magickalspot.com/signs-spirit-guide-contacting-you/?srsltid=AfmBOoo2JuZ47-ONs19rGrJX4M_kqlJbh6a4PN6D4lGVmrefVFjOeEn_

Cherry, K. (2020, May 13). *What is consciousness?* Verywell Mind. https://www.verywellmind.com/what-is-consciousness-2795922

Chrysalis, P. (2019, February 28). *B The Vibe.* B the Vibe. https://www.bthevibe.com/articles/2019/2/28/astral-projection-and-lucid-dreaming-basics

Dazed. (2023, August 16). *Astral projection: a guide to travelling to the astral realm.* Dazed. https://www.dazeddigital.com/beauty/article/60582/1/a-trip-to-the-astral-realm-dazed-astral-projection-travel-guide

Detori, E. (2012, August 4). *The dos and don'ts of Astral Projection*. The New Indian Express. https://www.newindianexpress.com/lifestyle/spirituality/2012/aug/05/the-dos-and-donts-of-astral-projection-393870.html

Dr. Tara Salay. (2021, March 31). *Energy Block In The Body - Relationship To Muscle Tightness*. Dr. Tara Salay. https://drtarasalay.com/energy-block-in-the-body/

Emelianov, D. (2023). *Mindful Space Clearing: A Comprehensive Guide*. Trimbox.io. https://www.trimbox.io/blog/mindful-space-clearing

Emma. (2021, February 27). *astral-projection and why everyone is doing it - Emma - Medium*. Medium. https://emmabee77.medium.com/astral-projection-and-why-everyone-is-doing-it-3c391b81378e

Essential oils for meditation - Saje Natural Wellness. (2024). Saje.com. https://www.saje.com/blogs/essential-oils-101/the-most-relaxing-essential-oils-for-meditation?srsltid=AfmBOoonqRgpBzcUhQ1zvlEuPMexdtKdgvCdNwmd26_Q83Tub11cwG3

Jayadev, T. (2012, November 3). *Liberating the Body from Energy Blockages*. Ananda. https://www.ananda.org/ask/liberating-the-body-from-energy-blockages/

Getting Started with Astral Projection» Grandma's Grimoire. (2023, September 27). Grandmas Grimoire. https://grandmasgrimoire.com/astral-projection/

GoddessLifestylePlan. (2013, June 2). *How To Call Upon Your Spirit Guides And Guardian Angels*. The Goddess Lifestyle Plan® | Life and Business Coaching. https://goddesslifestyleplan.com/how-to-call-upon-your-spirit-guides-and-guardian-angels/

Hands-On Meditation. (2020, January 15). *4-7-8 Calm Breathing Exercise - Relaxing Breath Technique | Hands-On Meditation*. Www.youtube.com. https://www.youtube.com/watch?v=1Dv-ldGLnIY

Hannah, D. (2024, April 10). *My Experiences With Astral Projection | Exploring The Hidden Realms Within*. Medium; http://symbosity.com/. https://medium.com/http-symbosity-com/my-experiences-with-astral-projection-exploring-the-hidden-realms-within-04f2d417e40b

Health benefits of gratitude. (2023, March 22). Www.uclahealth.org. https://www.uclahealth.org/news/article/health-benefits-gratitude

How To Prepare For Astral Projection. (n.d.). FasterCapital. https://fastercapital.com/topics/how-to-prepare-for-astral-projection.html

How to teach Healing Temple Meditation Pose - GeorgeWatts.org. (2020, December 5). GeorgeWatts.org; Lesson Planner. https://georgewatts.org/lesson-planner/yoga_pilates_poses/healing-temple/

How. (2023, April 20). *Adventuring with Poseidon.* Adventuring with Poseidon. https://www.adventuringwithposeidon.com/blog/how-to-release-emotional-overwhelm-energetic-blocks-meditation-tips

https://www.facebook.com/TanyaRichardsonBlessings. (2021). *mindbodygreen.* Mindbodygreen.com. https://www.mindbodygreen.com/articles/types-of-spirit-guides?srsltid=AfmBOoq2R5kOPfivffohya3dQvss-pP7ZGJXxTc_Adjr0x4Oqb2Cvwq1

Insight Network, Inc. (2024). *Insight Timer - #1 Free Meditation App for Sleep, Relax & More.* Insighttimer.com. https://insighttimer.com/fredrikstangeland/guided-meditations/meet-your-spirit-guide-astral-projection-meditation

Jordan. (2016, January 4). *Concentration/Visualization of an Object - Remembering The Gnostic Movement.* Remembering the Gnostic Movement. https://rememberingthegnosticmovement.com/practices/concentrationvisualization-practices/concentrationvisualization-of-an-object/?cn-reloaded=1

Joylina Admin. (2022, January 30). *The Seven Layers of the Aura.* Joylina.com. https://joylina.com/knowledgebase/healing/auras/seven-layers-of-the-aura

Krish Murali Eswar. (2023, June 8). *My Astral Travel Experiences That No One Talks About - Krish Murali Eswar.* Krish Murali Eswar. https://krishmuralieswar.com/my-astral-travel-experiences-that-no-one-talks-about/

Larkin, B. (2023). *Astral Projection: The Ultimate Guide for Beginners.* Tiny Rituals. https://tinyrituals.co/blogs/tiny-rituals/astral-projection?srsltid=AfmBOoqyF-BjuWlmXBa0Z9Tk2mVFzvjO4Au8udCORrDFa82QkL9KH-px

Lewis, R. (2023, November 25). *An Overview of the Leading Theories of Consciousness.* Psychology Today. https://www.psychologytoday.com/intl/blog/finding-purpose/202308/an-overview-of-the-leading-theories-of-consciousness

Little, G. (2022, March 3). *Archangel Michael Prayer for Protection - Illuminations!* Illuminations! https://illuminationscenter.com/2022/03/03/archangel-michael-prayer-for-protection/

MacIntyre, B. (2016, July 15). *How to Create and Reinforce Energetic & Spiritual Boundaries.* Brenda MacIntyre, Medicine Song Woman. https://medicinesongwoman.com/how-to-create-reinforce-energetic-spiritual-boundaries

Marossero, D. (2023, September 6). *Journeying beyond: My first "voluntary" travel to other realms through Astral Projection.* Medium.

https://dorotheemarossero.medium.com/journeying-beyond-my-first-voluntary-travel-to-other-realms-through-astral-projection-d41a07f40086

Michelle. (2022, May 23). *How Can the Astral Body Heal the Physical Body?* Ananda. https://www.ananda.org/ask/how-can-the-astral-body-heal-the-physical-body/

Pavlina, E. (2008, August 25). *How do I protect myself and my room when I astral project? • Erin Pavlina, Intuitive Counselor.* Erin Pavlina, Intuitive Counselor. https://www.erinpavlina.com/blog/2008/08/how-do-i-protect-myself-and-my-room-when-i-astral-project/

Pavlina, E. (2021, April 20). *Which is Better? Lucid Dreaming or Astral Projection? • Erin Pavlina, Intuitive Counselor.* Erin Pavlina, Intuitive Counselor. https://www.erinpavlina.com/blog/2021/04/which-is-better-lucid-dreaming-or-astral-projection/

Pavlina, S. (2006, July 9). *Ask Steve – Astral Projection – Steve Pavlina.* Stevepavlina.com. https://stevepavlina.com/blog/2006/07/ask-steve-astral-projection/

Qigong with Kseny. (2020, June 17). *8 Minute Practice To Ground Yourself and Feel Centered.* YouTube. https://www.youtube.com/watch?v=tQtH-GxQ8j8

Reid, S. (2022, June 6). *Gratitude: The Benefits and How to Practice It - HelpGuide.org.* HelpGuide.org. https://www.helpguide.org/mental-health/wellbeing/gratitude

Rose, M. (2024, May 20). *Astral Projection: How to Have an Out-of-Body Experience in 7 Easy Steps.* StyleCaster. https://stylecaster.com/lists/astral-projection/meditate-align-your-chakras/

SenGupta, D. (2020, April 30). *mindbodygreen.* Mindbodygreen.com. https://www.mindbodygreen.com/articles/how-to-ground-heal-balance-your-energy-levels?srsltid=AfmBOoonZsp8OXcik83iBvOv-3njL5aPFbKA_w8XUcEsBsXvak7ADalr

Sipos, E. (2023, December 14). *The History and Importance of How to Astral Project Safely.* AOV Crystals. https://aovcrystals.com/how-to-astral-project-safely/

Smookler, E. (2019, April 11). *Beginner's body scan meditation.* Mindful. https://www.mindful.org/beginners-body-scan-meditation/

Soul Journeys: Understanding Astral Projection - Matt Fraser. (2024, October 5). Meet Matt Fraser. https://meetmattfraser.com/167550-2/

The Alchemical Oracle (LiveLikeLo). (2022, September 1). *5 Steps To Create Your Sacred Space In The Astral /Astral Altars Series/ LiveLikeLo.* YouTube. https://www.youtube.com/watch?v=WbBzTZDWpDc

The Benefits Of Astral Projection - FasterCapital. (2024). FasterCapital. https://fastercapital.com/topics/the-benefits-of-astral-projection.html

Traversa, E. (2022, January 4). *How to Induce the Hypnagogic State.* Linkedin.com. https://www.linkedin.com/pulse/how-induce-hypnogogic-state-edward-traversa/

Turner, R. (2016). *The Startling Truth About Astral Projection (it's not real).* World-of-Lucid-Dreaming.com. https://www.world-of-lucid-dreaming.com/astral-projection.html

Vale, L. (2024, January 7). *Journey to Oneness: My First Astral Projection and the Art of Self-Discovery.* Medium. https://medium.com/@loredanavale33/journey-to-oneness-myfirst-astral-projection-and-the-art-of-self-discovery-c253980058ae

Virtued Academy International. (2023, November 27). Virtued.in. https://www.virtued.in/blog/benefits-of-astral-projection-enhancing-spiritual-growth-and-self-discovery

Visualization Techniques – – Ambient Sound Healing. (2014). *Ambient Sound Healing.* Ambient Sound Healing. https://ambientsoundhealing.com/astral-projection-1/online-presence-4bdpp-7gcnx-8pzeh-4c9bc-hbfyf

Image Sources

1 Designed by Freepik, https://www.freepik.com/free-photo/fantasy-astral-wallpaper-composition_39425681.htm#fromView=search&page=1&position=17&uuid=13e8a39e-67a5-4776-89fc-fddc2c0371aa&query=astral
2 The free media repository., CC BY-SA 2.5 <https://creativecommons.org/licenses/by-sa/2.5>, via Wikimedia Commons https://commons.wikimedia.org/wiki/File:091717-34-Descartes-Philosophy.jpg
3 https://www.pexels.com/photo/woman-in-yellow-jacket-and-blue-denim-jeans-sitting-on-blue-round-inflatable-ring-6931924/
4 https://www.pexels.com/photo/a-glass-bottles-near-the-wooden-box-and-flowers-3865680/
5 https://www.pexels.com/photo/woman-in-white-shirt-holding-orange-and-white-lollipop-6943953/
6 https://www.pexels.com/photo/woman-meditating-with-candles-and-incense-3822864/
7 https://www.pexels.com/photo/person-holding-notebook-beside-ceramic-cup-1541216/
8 https://www.pexels.com/photo/woman-in-black-top-sitting-on-brown-armchair-3331574/
9 https://www.pexels.com/photo/woman-wearing-black-sleeveless-dress-holding-white-headphone-at-daytime-1001850/
10 https://www.pexels.com/photo/close-up-photo-of-crystal-stones-on-a-person-s-hand-6954663/
11 https://www.pexels.com/photo/man-wearing-black-cap-with-eyes-closed-under-cloudy-sky-810775/
12 https://www.pexels.com/photo/man-wearing-green-t-shirt-and-white-shorts-2463079/
13 https://www.pexels.com/photo/silhouette-photo-of-woman-during-dawn-1835016/
14 https://www.pexels.com/photo/photo-of-woman-writing-on-notebook-3059749/
15 https://www.pexels.com/photo/close-up-photo-of-glowing-blue-butterflies-326055/

16 https://www.pexels.com/photo/woman-practicing-yoga-with-closed-eyes-12603755/
17 https://www.pexels.com/photo/grayscale-photography-of-angel-statue-under-cloudy-skies-208001/
18 https://www.pexels.com/photo/positive-young-woman-meditating-with-closed-eyes-4498281/

www.ingramcontent.com/pod-product-compliance
Lightning Source LLC
Chambersburg PA
CBHW051847160426
43209CB00006B/1196